Acting Edition

Agatha Christie's The Mirror Crack'd

A New Adaptation by
Rachel Wagstaff

THE MIRROR CRACK'D © 2022 Agatha Christie Limited.
All rights reserved.

Adapted from
THE MIRROR CRACK'D FROM SIDE TO SIDE
© 1962 Agatha Christie Limited. All rights reserved.

AGATHA CHRISTIE, MARPLE, the Agatha Christie Signature and the AC Monogram Logo are registered trademarks of Agatha Christie Limited in the UK and elsewhere.
All rights reserved.

THE MIRROR CRACK'D is fully protected under the copyright laws of the United States of America, the British Commonwealth, including Canada, and all member countries of the Berne Convention for the Protection of Literary and Artistic Works, the Universal Copyright Convention, and/or the World Trade Organization conforming to the Agreement on Trade Related Aspects of Intellectual Property Rights. All rights, including professional and amateur stage productions, recitation, lecturing, public reading, motion picture, radio broadcasting, television, online/digital production, and the rights of translation into foreign languages are strictly reserved.

ISBN 978-0-573-71098-8

www.concordtheatricals.com
www.concordtheatricals.co.uk

FOR PRODUCTION INQUIRIES

UNITED STATES AND CANADA
info@concordtheatricals.com
1-866-979-0447

UNITED KINGDOM AND EUROPE
licensing@concordtheatricals.co.uk
020-7054-7298

Each title is subject to availability from Concord Theatricals Corp., depending upon country of performance. Please be aware that *THE MIRROR CRACK'D* may not be licensed by Concord Theatricals Corp. in your territory. Professional and amateur producers should contact the nearest Concord Theatricals Corp. office or licensing partner to verify availability.

CAUTION: Professional and amateur producers are hereby warned that *THE MIRROR CRACK'D* is subject to a licensing fee. The purchase, renting, lending or use of this book does not constitute a license to perform this title(s), which license must be obtained from Concord Theatricals Corp. prior to any performance. Performance of this title(s) without a license is a violation of federal law and may subject the producer and/or presenter of such performances to civil penalties. Both amateurs and professionals considering a production are strongly advised to apply to the appropriate agent before starting rehearsals, advertising, or booking a theatre. A licensing fee must be paid whether the title(s) is presented for charity or gain and whether or not admission is charged. Professional/Stock licensing fees are quoted upon application to Concord Theatricals Corp.

This work is published by Samuel French, an imprint of Concord Theatricals Corp.

No one shall make any changes in this title(s) for the purpose of production. No part of this book may be reproduced, stored in a retrieval system, scanned, uploaded, or transmitted in any form, by any means, now known or yet to be invented, including mechanical, electronic, digital, photocopying, recording, videotaping, or otherwise, without the prior written permission of the publisher. No one shall share this title(s), or any part of this title(s), through any social media or file hosting websites.

For all inquiries regarding motion picture, television, online/digital and other media rights, please contact Concord Theatricals Corp.

MUSIC AND THIRD-PARTY MATERIALS USE NOTE

Licensees are solely responsible for obtaining formal written permission from copyright owners to use copyrighted music and/or other copyrighted third-party materials (e.g. artworks, logos) in the performance of this play and are strongly cautioned to do so. If no such permission is obtained by the licensee, then the licensee must use only original music and materials that the licensee owns and controls. Licensees are solely responsible and liable for clearances of all third-party copyrighted materials, including without limitation music, and shall indemnify the copyright owners of the play(s) and their licensing agent, Concord Theatricals Corp., against any costs, expenses, losses and liabilities arising from the use of such copyrighted third-party materials by licensees. For music, please contact the appropriate music licensing authority in your territory for the rights to any incidental music.

IMPORTANT BILLING AND CREDIT REQUIREMENTS

If you have obtained performance rights to this title, please refer to your licensing agreement for important billing and credit requirements.

THE MIRROR CRACK'D premiered at Salisbury Playhouse on 15 February 2019, followed by a UK tour. It was a Wales Millennium Centre and Wiltshire Creative co-production, directed by Melly Still. Original Theatre then toured the UK with a new production, directed by Philip Franks, from October 2022 to February 2023.

SALISBURY PLAYHOUSE CAST:

MISS JANE MARPLE	Susie Blake
CHERRY BAKER	Katie Matsell
CHIEF INSPECTOR DERMOT CRADDOCK	Simon Shepherd
HEATHER LEIGH	Katherine Manners
CYRIL LEIGH	Colin R Campbell
DOLLY BANTRY	Julia Hills
MARINA GREGG	Suzanna Hamilton
JASON RUDD	Joe Dixon
ELLA ZIELINSKY	Davina Moon
LOLA BREWSTER	Gillian Saker
GIUSEPPE RENZO	Huw Parmenter

ORIGINAL THEATRE CAST:

MISS JANE MARPLE	Susie Blake
CHERRY BAKER	Mara Allen
CHIEF INSPECTOR DERMOT CRADDOCK	Oliver Boot
HEATHER LEIGH	Jules Mevin
CYRIL LEIGH	David Partridge
DOLLY BANTRY	Veronica Roberts
MARINA GREGG	Sophie Ward
JASON RUDD	Joe McFadden
ELLA ZIELINSKY	Sarah Lawrie
LOLA BREWSTER	Chrystine Symone
GIUSEPPE RENZO	Lorenzo Martelli

CHARACTERS

MISS JANE MARPLE
CHERRY BAKER
CHIEF INSPECTOR DERMOT CRADDOCK
HEATHER LEIGH
CYRIL LEIGH
DOLLY BANTRY
MARINA GREGG
JASON RUDD
ELLA ZIELINSKY
LOLA BREWSTER
GIUSEPPE RENZO

Other parts are played by members of the company

SETTING

St Mary Mead, a little English village. The village has always been a sleepy, respectable place but has recently been modernised with a new development, to the horror of the older inhabitants. Even more recently, the village has been thrown into a frenzy by the news that the Manor House has been bought by a famous couple from Hollywood.

TIME

July 1962

NOTES ON SCRIPT

/ indicates where a line overlaps
... indicates a trailing off, or a pause for thought
– indicates an interruption

ADAPTOR'S NOTE

The first play I ever (co-) wrote was with Isabella Sharp. We were both eight at the time and best friends at primary school. We called the play *Never Two Without Three* and, as our title might reveal, it was a clumsy homage to an Agatha Christie short story (a Miss Marple, of course. For me, it was always Miss Marple).

Our only audience was Izy's patient mother. Perhaps the real wonder is that it has taken me so many years to dramatise my second Miss Marple. My own beloved mother has most (all?) of Agatha Christie's books and I think I had read every single one before I was ten! It was a much-loved family ritual, for us all to settle down to Joan Hickson's Miss Marple or to David Suchet's Poirot at the weekend. Even the opening few notes to either theme tune instantly takes me back to that living room, and the thrill of anticipation of a world gone by where good (nearly) always triumphs. My teacher was less than impressed when I wrote in my school diary that watching "Sleeping Murder" had given me nightmares... but I was not to be deterred and so hid that particular reprimand from my parents, for as long as I could. Till now, perhaps! So when I was first approached by Nick Frankfort (to Nick, huge thanks) to adapt *The Mirror Crack'd*, I was as delighted as I was apprehensive. To have loved something for so long makes you very aware of how much it must mean to others too. But it has been such a pleasure, working on this incredible story over many years, on and off! Having the generous support of Agatha Christie's grandson, Mathew Prichard, and, more latterly, great-grandson, James Prichard, has felt akin to having the blessing of Agatha Christie herself. Many thanks to James, Mathew and Lucy for their support, contributions and wonderful warmth and hospitality over the years. I am also deeply indebted to Julia Wilde at ACL, who has been both brilliant and incredibly supportive throughout. To Julia and to all at ACL, sincere gratitude.

The Mirror Crack'd has always had a special place in my heart. I can't say why without what would be called a "spoiler alert" but it was a story that resonated deeply with my family. The typical brilliance of Christie's plotting combined with such a compelling motive has been a real gift. I knew right away that I wanted to play and re-play the murder from different perspectives as characters conjure up what they remember, or claim to remember, for an out-of-action Miss Marple. I also wanted to delve deeper into Jane Marple herself, a character who has always fascinated me.

An older lady, sidelined both metaphorically and literally in this case; an underestimated "spinster", who had the bad luck to live during a time when she could never have been a Chief Inspector of Scotland Yard and yet, just happened to be the most astute of us all... Inevitably, I have had to elide certain characters to make it work on stage, also re-ordering events where necessary to make sure that key characters get to meet in the denouement but, at every stage, I have endeavoured to be true to my favourite of Agatha Christie's extraordinary thrillers.

I am hugely indebted to Melly Still, who originally dramaturged the play and directed the original production, for her self-declared forensic approach, dedication and care. Likewise to Philip Franks, who directed the second production. His intelligence, knowledge and sensitivity meant the process was a joy throughout. You always learn a great deal from watching a show on stage, particularly from listening to the audience, and I have very much enjoyed reworking the show for, during and after both productions!

Speaking of productions, many thanks to Pádraig Cusack, the Wales Millennium Centre and Wiltshire Creative for the first production and for taking it to NCPA in Mumbai. Sincere thanks too to Alastair Whatley and to his Original Theatre company, for breathing fresh life into the play with their UK tour.

I would also like to thank the team at Concord, particularly Steven Greenhalgh, Emma Anacootee and Ben Keiper, for their excellent work.

Grateful thanks too to the casts and crews from each workshop and production. Your insights, generosity of spirit and talent helped to bring the script to life as it evolved over the years.

And finally, heartfelt thanks to my family and friends for their support throughout; likewise, to my writer pals, Mike Bartlett and Sam Adamson, and to my brilliant agent, Dan Usztan, who might love Agatha Christie even more than I do!

Rachel Wagstaff, April 2024

ACT ONE

Scene One

(1962. Sunday morning. Late July.)

*(**MISS MARPLE** sleeps in her chair, a blanket over her. Her ankle is bandaged.)*

(We see Miss Marple's dream, in which Marina Gregg appears, trapped in a glass box.)

*(**MARINA** steps out of the box. Every inch the Hollywood star. Out of reach.)*

(Police sirens, morphing into the sound of a telephone ringing.)

*(**MISS MARPLE** wakes. She tries to get up but suddenly feels the pain of her ankle.)*

MISS MARPLE. Oh, bugger!

Cherry?

*(**MISS MARPLE** looks at her watch.)*

Cherry?!

(The telephone stops ringing.)

(Silence.)

(The telephone rings again. **MISS MARPLE** *tries to get up again but she can't.)*

(The telephone stops ringing. **MISS MARPLE** *tries to retrieve her bag but it's out of reach. As are her crutches. Suddenly, the sound of the front door opening, slamming shut.)*

MISS MARPLE. Cherry? Is that you?

*(***CHERRY*** rushes in.)*

CHERRY. Sorry I'm late.

I can't think of an excuse.

(Taking off her coat.) Were you all right, on your own?

MISS MARPLE. Of course.

CHERRY. I was worried about you. Stuck down here all night.

MISS MARPLE. It made a nice change.

CHERRY. I'll do your bandage first, shall I? And then I'll do your face.

MISS MARPLE. I'm not an invalid.

I couldn't reach my bag, that's all.

CHERRY. Oh. Sorry.

*(***CHERRY*** fetches Miss Marple's bag.)*

Won't be a sec.

*(***CHERRY*** goes.* **MISS MARPLE** *takes out her powder. Powders her face. She suddenly notices the silence.)*

*(***CHERRY*** returns, holding a bandage.)*

MISS MARPLE. Is something wrong?

CHERRY. Eh?

MISS MARPLE. Usually, you sing, as you dash around.

CHERRY. Do I?

You should've said, if you minded.

MISS MARPLE. I don't mind.

CHERRY. Right.

>(**CHERRY** *sits to change* **MISS MARPLE**'s *bandage.*)

Does it hurt?

>(**CHERRY** *is yanking* **MISS MARPLE**'s *foot onto a stool.*)

MISS MARPLE. Only when you do that!

CHERRY. Sorry. I'm all fingers and thumbs today.

MISS MARPLE. You're doing a splendid job.

Did you get to see her?

CHERRY. Who?

MISS MARPLE. Marina Gregg.

CHERRY. Oh! Yeah. Yeah, I did.

MISS MARPLE. Is she really as lovely as they say?

CHERRY. …S'funny. Being so close, I couldn't really look at her.

MISS MARPLE. I dreamt about her last night. I dreamt…

CHERRY. *(Genuinely interested.)* What?

MISS MARPLE. Forgive me. Other people's dreams are even more tiresome than other people's holiday slides.

I did see Miss Gregg onstage once, though. Years ago. I'll never forget it.

CHERRY. What was the play?

MISS MARPLE. I don't remember.

Oh, of course. It was *A Doll's House*. You get so caught up with how very trapped Nora feels that you'd forgive her almost anything. And yet, to walk out on your children…

CHERRY. I've never seen it.

Right. I'll get yer breakfast.

> (**CHERRY** *leaves.*)
>
> (*Silence.*)
>
> (**CHERRY** *returns.*)

I thought I'd push the boat out and do your eggs boiled today.

MISS MARPLE. Lovely.

CHERRY. Oh! I forgot your tea.

Sorry. I'm at sixes and sevens today.

MISS MARPLE. Are you all right?

CHERRY. Sorry, Miss, it's just…

MISS MARPLE. What's happened?

> (*Pause.*)

CHERRY. I know it's daft but whenever something bad happens… I lost my sister, a few years ago now, mind, and… but it's still her I want to tell, and then, it's like I've lost her, all over again.

MISS MARPLE. Yes.

Grief, it casts such terribly long shadows.

(Beat.)

CHERRY. Them eggs'll be done by now.

*(**CHERRY** goes.)*

(Silence.)

*(**CHERRY** returns.)*

The eggs have only gone and cracked! I'll have to start again.

MISS MARPLE. Actually, I'm not hungry.

Losing a sister as a child must be terribly lonely.

CHERRY. The thing is, I don't know if I'm making a memory from a photograph or if I actually remember her. I can't even remember what it was like to be held by her, or if she even – sorry. Here's me harping on, and you got enough on your plate, what with your gammy leg…

MISS MARPLE. I've plenty of time to listen.

(Silence.)

CHERRY. It's just, I don't know anyone round here and…

MISS MARPLE. What's happened, dear?

CHERRY. …I dunno…

MISS MARPLE. You've been here a week. How many people have called round in all that time?

CHERRY. …?

MISS MARPLE. If you have a secret that's troubling you… I've no one to tell.

CHERRY. It must be 'orrible, being old.

Not that you're…

MISS MARPLE. I've never felt "old" before. But being stuck in this chair...

It's an awful thing, Cherry dear, to feel alone with your cares.

Tell me what's upset you.

CHERRY. ...It was at the drinks party yesterday. You see –

(The sound of the doorbell.)

MISS MARPLE. It's probably just a travelling salesman. Go on.

CHERRY. Well, thing is –

(The doorbell rings again. Then the sound of the front door opening. **CHIEF INSPECTOR DERMOT CRADDOCK** *appears.* **CHERRY** *intercepts him.)*

Sorry, can I help you?

CRADDOCK. I'm looking for Miss Marple –

MISS MARPLE. Dermot! What a lovely surprise.

CRADDOCK. You're always so quick to the door. I thought something must have happened to you.

MISS MARPLE. I had a silly fall. This is Cherry. She's been looking after me. Cherry, this is Inspector Craddock.

CHERRY. Inspector...?

MISS MARPLE. His parents were friends of mine.

CRADDOCK. Chief Inspector now, actually!

MISS MARPLE. Oh.

CRADDOCK. What?

MISS MARPLE. No. That's very good news. Just like your father.

(Beat.)

CHERRY. You sure you don't want them eggs?

MISS MARPLE. Perhaps just the tea, dear. And we can talk, again, later…?

>   (**MISS MARPLE** *smiles gently at* **CHERRY**. *Beat.* **CHERRY** *leaves.*)

CRADDOCK. How bad is it?

MISS MARPLE. Just a sprain.

CRADDOCK. At least you're being looked after.

MISS MARPLE. My nephew insisted on paying for some help… The trouble is, these days, girls aren't trained. Faithful Florence. There was a parlourmaid for you.

CRADDOCK. Why don't you ask her back?

MISS MARPLE. Faithful Florence is fifty-five and has gout.

CRADDOCK. I can't get used to girls in trousers.

>   (**MISS MARPLE** *raises an eyebrow. Craddock so behind the times.*)

MISS MARPLE. What's happened?

CRADDOCK. Can't I just come to see you?

MISS MARPLE. It was at the drinks party.

CRADDOCK. What have you heard?

MISS MARPLE. Nothing, yet.

CRADDOCK. You don't by any chance know a Mrs Heather Leigh?

MISS MARPLE. Has something happened to her?

CRADDOCK. So, you did know her? I thought she was from the dreaded Development.

(**CHERRY** *has entered, carrying a tray. She puts it down emphatically.*)

MISS MARPLE. Thank you, Cherry.

(*Frostily,* **CHERRY** *pours the tea, hands them both a cup. She puts the tea cosy back on the pot, leaves.*)

...Cherry lives on the Development. Dolly thinks I'm mad – not that she's met Cherry yet, but... You remember Dolly Bantry. She and the Colonel owned Gossington Hall. Actually, I'm not sure Dolly's quite forgiven you for accusing her husband of murder.

CRADDOCK. We found the body of a young girl in his library!

MISS MARPLE. If you bludgeoned a young lady to death, would you leave her lying in your library?

CRADDOCK. Well. We cleared it up nicely in the end.

MISS MARPLE. Yes. We did.

CRADDOCK. You were saying, you knew Heather Leigh?

MISS MARPLE. I was going for a quiet walk, minding my own business, when –

CRADDOCK. You just happened to walk past the Development.

MISS MARPLE. (*Smiles wryly.*) It was my own fault. I didn't see the loose paving stone –

(**MISS MARPLE** *falls.* **HEATHER LEIGH** *appears. Back in time a week, the scene reconstructed.*)

HEATHER. Here, let me help you.

MISS MARPLE. It's my ankle.

(**HEATHER** *examines it.*)

HEATHER. It's not broken. Well, that's a relief! You old folk do suffer with your bones. I should know, with my training. I'm the new chair of the local branch of St John Ambulance. Heather Leigh. I expect you've heard of me.

MISS MARPLE. I'm afraid I –

HEATHER. Come and have a nice cup of tea, and then my husband will run you home.

> (**MISS MARPLE** *tries to get up. It's too painful.* **HEATHER** *intercedes.*)

You just stay put, dear, and I'll see to it.

(Calling.) Cyril! Cyril! Put the kettle on!

What's your name?

MISS MARPLE. Jane Marple. I'm from the village.

HEATHER. Oooh! Are you going to the drinks party at Gossington Hall?

MISS MARPLE. I'm afraid I haven't been invited.

HEATHER. I'm going on behalf of St John Ambulance. I'll be so nervous, mingling with all those stars, I expect I won't be able to get a word out!

MISS MARPLE. I'm sure you'll manage.

Thank you for looking after me.

HEATHER. Anyone would have done the same.

Cyril! Cyril!

Honestly, that man...

> (**CYRIL LEIGH** *appears with a tray.* **HEATHER** *takes it from him.*)

(Adding sugar to a cup.) Four sugars should do the trick –

MISS MARPLE. Actually, I don't take –

HEATHER. Sugar's terribly good for the shock. Now, you get that down you and you'll be right as rain.

> (**MISS MARPLE** *takes a sip. Tries not to grimace. She turns back to* **CRADDOCK**.)

MISS MARPLE. Heather Leigh was kindness itself, though she only saw the world from her point of view...

> (**HEATHER** *leaves with the tray. Taking the cup from* **MISS MARPLE** *as she goes.* **MISS MARPLE** *and* **HEATHER** *exchange a small smile.*)

I suppose she is dead.

CRADDOCK. You know I'm not allowed to...

MISS MARPLE. One always suspects the husband first but –

> (*We see* **CYRIL** *again, helping* **MISS MARPLE** *into her chair.*)

CYRIL. The doctor's on his way.

MISS MARPLE. Thank you.

You've been very kind. You and your wife.

CYRIL. That's my Heather. She'd do anything for anyone. Whether they like it or not!

> (*They smile.*)

Do you have someone to look after you?

MISS MARPLE. I'll call my nephew. Raymond. He's very good to me. He's a writer, and he's made a fortune on his books – so...

CYRIL. Of course.

> (**CYRIL** *lingers.*)

I used to read.

MISS MARPLE. Oh yes?

CYRIL. Poetry, mostly.

Is there anything else you need?

CRADDOCK. Sounds a peaceable chap.

MISS MARPLE. I wonder why he stopped reading?

CRADDOCK. Anyway, not the murdering sort.

(**CYRIL** *disappears.*)

MISS MARPLE. But I can't see why anyone would want to kill Heather Leigh… Ah.

CRADDOCK. What?

MISS MARPLE. You think it was the wrong murder.

CRADDOCK. What makes you say that?

MISS MARPLE. Why would Scotland Yard send a *Chief Inspector* to investigate the murder of a middle-aged nobody?

(*Beat.*)

How was she killed?

CRADDOCK. You know that I'm not at liberty to discuss the case.

MISS MARPLE. So why are you here?

CRADDOCK. I thought I'd pop in, as I was in the village.

MISS MARPLE. At eight o'clock in the morning?

CRADDOCK. Old people are early risers.

MISS MARPLE. It's because we've so much to pack into our days.

CRADDOCK. Feeling a little sorry for yourself?

MISS MARPLE. Feeling a little patronising?

Dermot. I held you when you were three days old.

(Beat.)

CRADDOCK. Traces of a drug were discovered in Heather Leigh's strawberry daiquiri.

MISS MARPLE. A strawberry daiquiri?

CRADDOCK. It's a cocktail.

MISS MARPLE. I meant, I wouldn't have had Heather Leigh down as the daiquiri type.

What kind of drug?

CRADDOCK. Twelve times the prescribed dose of a "die-ethyl..."

MISS MARPLE. Diethylbarbiturate. It goes by the trade name – / Calmo.

CRADDOCK. Calmo. / How do you know it?

MISS MARPLE. I did work in a pharmacy.

CRADDOCK. When?

MISS MARPLE. And this was at the drinks party yesterday?

CRADDOCK. Yes, at Gossington Hall.

MISS MARPLE. Dolly was there. Dolly Bantry, you remember –

CRADDOCK. Yes, I remember Dolly bloody Bantry! Has she told you anything?

MISS MARPLE. No...no, she hasn't.

(Silence.)

CRADDOCK. Well then...

MISS MARPLE. I presume you believe Marina Gregg to be the intended victim.

CRADDOCK. ...

MISS MARPLE. I must say, it struck me as very strange when Dolly told me that Gossington Hall had been bought by Miss Marina Gregg. After all these years out of the limelight, why move to a little English village?

CRADDOCK. I never had you down as interested in the lives of Hollywood stars...though I suppose the village gossip grapevine must be positively self-combusting.

MISS MARPLE. Which is why you came here.

(Beat.)

CRADDOCK. Miss Gregg is making a motion picture at Hellingforth Studio. It's only a few miles from here...

MISS MARPLE. Yes, but why not Hollywood? I mean, one can't help wondering from what, or from whom, she is running.

CRADDOCK. Have you met her yet? Miss Gregg?

MISS MARPLE. No.

CRADDOCK. What about your friends?

MISS MARPLE. ...I'm afraid no one's called round much recently.

CRADDOCK. Too caught up with the excitement of Hollywood arriving on your doorstep.

MISS MARPLE. And the Development.

CRADDOCK. Yes. Rotten luck, that.

*(**CRADDOCK** goes to leave.)*

If there's anything I can do to help while I'm in the village. A library book, perhaps?

MISS MARPLE. If someone was actually after Miss Gregg, then I imagine that she is in terrible danger.

(**CRADDOCK** *kisses* **MISS MARPLE**.)

CRADDOCK. Goodbye, Aunt Jane.

MISS MARPLE. I wish you wouldn't call me that.

Is there anyone she suspects?

(Beat.)

CRADDOCK. I haven't managed to speak to her yet.

MISS MARPLE. Why not?

CRADDOCK. I only got here late last night.

MISS MARPLE. But you went straight to Gossington.

CRADDOCK. She'd already gone to bed.

MISS MARPLE. Yes, but surely…

CRADDOCK. Look. Jason Rudd – her husband – said Miss Gregg was in a delicate state.

(**JASON RUDD** *appears.*)

MISS MARPLE. You didn't like him.

CRADDOCK. What are you talking about?

MISS MARPLE. You get a twitch, right there –

CRADDOCK. No I don't.

MISS MARPLE. You did it again.

You saw something in him, didn't you?

CRADDOCK. He was very…

MISS MARPLE. Protective?

CRADDOCK. Belligerent.

MISS MARPLE. Ah. No respect for authority.

JASON. What d'you want?

CRADDOCK. Now, let me get this right. You're the film producer.

JASON. Director.

CRADDOCK. I'm so sorry. I always get the two muddled up. What's the difference?

JASON. The producer's the money. I'm the talent.

CRADDOCK. I thought the director just told the actors where to stand?

JASON. What did you say you wanted?

CRADDOCK. Chief Inspector Craddock. Scotland Yard.

JASON. And?

CRADDOCK. I'm here about the murder.

JASON. I've already spoken to the police.

CRADDOCK. The *local* police. I need to speak to your wife.

JASON. Why?

CRADDOCK. Mr Rudd, I realise this may come as something of a shock to you but it is possible that the poisoned daiquiri was intended for Miss Gregg.

JASON. What?

But who would want to kill Marina?

CRADDOCK. I was rather hoping you could tell me that. Does she have any enemies?

JASON. That's a very Biblical word.

CRADDOCK. Is there anyone your wife is afraid of?

JASON. Critics. But critics murder careers, not people.

CRADDOCK. Is there anyone whom your wife might have injured inadvertently? Perhaps a bad ending to one of her *five* other marriages?

JASON. All her divorces were amicable. *(At* **CRADDOCK**'s *raised eyebrow.)* Divorce is a common occurrence in Hollywood.

CRADDOCK. I can imagine… Now, as I said, I need to speak to Miss Gregg –

JASON. That's out of the question. My wife has collapsed with nervous exhaustion.

CRADDOCK. I'm sure she could manage a couple of questions.

JASON. When I met Marina, she was very unwell. I have dedicated the last eight years to nursing her back to health –

CRADDOCK. If someone tried to kill her, it seems highly likely that they will strike again –

JASON. Marina is the love of my life. I won't let any harm / come to her.

CRADDOCK. You don't think we should warn her that someone may be trying to / take her life?

JASON. You're not listening! That someone had to die here was bad enough. But if she found out that it was actually an attempt on *her* life –

CRADDOCK. Could you at least ask her if she'll speak to me –

JASON. She's my wife, Inspector, and if I say it's too soon to interrogate her – yes, *interrogate* her, then it's too soon.

CRADDOCK. …Is there something you're trying to conceal?

JASON. Do you think I'd admit to it if there was?

She'll be asleep right now, anyway.

CRADDOCK. And you're sure of that?

(Beat.)

JASON. Okay. Look. I gave her something to help her sleep.

CRADDOCK. What did you give her?

JASON. Calmo. Why?

CRADDOCK. Where'd you get it from?

JASON. I don't know. Ask Ella Zielinsky. Our secretary. Or Giuseppe Renzo. Our butler.

(**CRADDOCK** *writes in his notepad.*)

CRADDOCK. What does Calmo do?

JASON. It peps you up and it calms you down. (*Archly.*) You should try it.

(**CRADDOCK** *unimpressed.*)

Sorry. It's late and we've all had a shitty day, as I'm sure you can imagine. Come back tomorrow morning and we'll see if my wife is up to speaking to you.

CRADDOCK. One last thing. Do you have any idea how Mrs Leigh ended up with the poisoned drink?

JASON. I'm a director, not some damn waiter.

(**CRADDOCK** *turns back to* **MISS MARPLE**.)

CRADDOCK. Before you ask, the butler was serving the drinks. The aforementioned Giuseppe Renzo. (*Disapprovingly.*) Italian.

MISS MARPLE. Does his descent have any bearing on the case?

(*Beat.* **GIUSEPPE** *appears.*)

GIUSEPPE. Me? You accuse me?

CRADDOCK. All I asked was if it was correct that you served the drinks.

GIUSEPPE. Marina chose her drink herself, from a whole tray of drinks! So did Mrs Leigh!

CRADDOCK. Is there anyone who can vouch for that?

GIUSEPPE. Yes. Anyone who saw!

You think it was me. That's ridiculous! Why would I want to kill her?

I love Marina. Love.

Nineteen years, I follow her everywhere. I keep her safe, I keep her…clear. How could I try to kill that woman? She needs protecting. She needs tenderness, care. Like a flower. She needs –

CRADDOCK. Water and sunlight?

GIUSEPPE. You English, you have no heart.

(**GIUSEPPE** *disappears.*)

MISS MARPLE. Clear?

CRADDOCK. From fans, I suppose. Newspapers. Photographers. Everyone wanting to catch a glimpse of her…

MISS MARPLE. Yes, but it's such an unusual choice of word.

CRADDOCK. Well. I should –

MISS MARPLE. How much would Mr Rudd stand to inherit if Miss Gregg died?

(**CRADDOCK** *consults his notepad.* **JASON** *appears again.*)

JASON. Two million dollars.

MISS MARPLE. It seems too obvious.

CRADDOCK. I've already looked into all that. If the film collapsed, he'd stand to lose –

JASON. Considerably more.

MISS MARPLE. Why would he admit to giving his wife Calmo if he knew that was how Heather Leigh was killed?

CRADDOCK. Unless it's a very clever double bluff. The man certainly has guts, I'll give him that.

(**JASON** *eyeballs* **CRADDOCK**. *Toasts him. Leaves.*)

Now, I really ought to get back to – [Gossington]

(**DOLLY** *appears.* **CHERRY** *running after her.*)

CHERRY. She said she always lets herself in –

DOLLY. Jane, you'll never guess –

MISS MARPLE. Dolly! Dolly, this is Cherry. Cherry, Mrs Bantry, one of my dearest friends.

(**DOLLY** *looks at* **CHERRY**. *Alarmed.*)

CHERRY. Hi.

(**CHERRY** *goes.*)

DOLLY. Oh, Jane. Cherry's not even a real name! She'll probably suffocate you in your sleep and make off with the silver!

(**CRADDOCK** *stifles a laugh.*)

Oh. I didn't see you there.

MISS MARPLE. You remember Inspector Craddock. Dolly Bantry.

CRADDOCK. A pleasure to see you again, Mrs Bantry.

DOLLY. *(To* **MISS MARPLE.***)* I would have come last night but I was looking after poor Cyril Leigh. Oh, Jane. I had to walk through the Development, on my own! And you should have seen it –

MISS MARPLE. Yes, I have been – [there]

DOLLY. Rows and rows of bland little boxes, all with fences made of chicken wire! And as for the people – men in tight trousers, and young gels, pushing prams, and not a wedding ring in sight! I mean, really. Oh – and right at the end, you'll never guess. A *Super Market*!

MISS MARPLE. How was Mr Leigh?

(CYRIL appears. Devastated.)

DOLLY. I sat with him for hours, but what is there that can be said?

(CYRIL goes to speak. CRADDOCK turns back to DOLLY, cutting CYRIL off before he can say a word.)

CRADDOCK. Mrs Bantry. I believe you were at the drinks party. Did you see anything out of the ordinary?

DOLLY. Apart from that poor woman, dropping down dead, you mean? What was it? A stroke? Heart attack?

CRADDOCK. No one rushed to her aid?

DOLLY. We all did. But there was nothing to be done.

CRADDOCK. So, you saw nothing suspicious. Nothing of use.

DOLLY. It seems not.

MISS MARPLE. *(To DOLLY.)* Tea?

DOLLY. Let me.

(DOLLY tops up MISS MARPLE's cup; pours herself a cup of tea. They both look at CRADDOCK.)

CRADDOCK. Well, I'll leave you ladies to it.

MISS MARPLE. *(To CRADDOCK.)* Do call again, Dermot, once you've tied it all up.

(**CRADDOCK** *leaves. Or pretends to leave. Instead he lingers, listens.*)

DOLLY. *(Conspirationally.)* I presume she was murdered!

MISS MARPLE. What makes you say that?

DOLLY. Why else would your *friend* be clumping around?

(**MISS MARPLE** *smiles. Begins to knit.*)

MISS MARPLE. It's funny. I only met Mrs Leigh once. If I'm honest, I didn't really take to her. But it's still such a pity... How little we know of when our own end will come.

DOLLY. She was rather bossy...

MISS MARPLE. I hope the murderer isn't on a spree. I'd have no friends left at all.

DOLLY. I'm not bossy.

(Beat.)

MISS MARPLE. Apparently, she had a strawberry daiquiri...?

DOLLY. So, she was poisoned?!

MISS MARPLE. Tell me exactly what you saw.

DOLLY. Heather Leigh was chattering away to Marina Gregg, and then someone sneezed and Heather Leigh must have startled and spilled her drink. Heather Leigh looked mortified but Marina played the gracious hostess and –

MISS MARPLE. Ah. Handed over her own drink.

DOLLY. Oh! Oh, I see! Heather Leigh was killed...but really someone was going for Marina Gregg!

MISS MARPLE. That poor woman.

DOLLY. She must be terrified they'll try again.

MISS MARPLE. I meant... [poor Heather]

DOLLY. Jane?

MISS MARPLE. Hmm? Never mind.

(Silence.)

Did you get to speak to Miss Gregg?

DOLLY. Actually, she'd invited me for tea, before the party!

MISS MARPLE. You didn't tell me.

DOLLY. It was just a courtesy cuppa. They had bought my home, after all. Oh, remind me to tell you about the Tennyson.

MISS MARPLE. Did you mind? Going back to Gossington...

DOLLY. Do you know, I thought I would, but once I met Marina... Oh, you should have seen her.

MISS MARPLE. What was she like?

*(**MARINA GREGG** appears. Loveliness itself.)*

MARINA. *(Greeting **DOLLY**.)* Mrs Bantry... This must be so difficult for you, seeing total strangers marching around your home.

DOLLY. Not at all. I'm so excited it's you!

MARINA. I *knew* I would like you. Your home, it has such character.

DOLLY. Your home now. I do hope you'll be happy here.

MARINA. I could feel it, even as we were coming up the drive: that at last, I had found somewhere peaceful, somewhere that I could be divinely happy.

*(**JASON** appears.)*

And meet most of the reason why. My beautiful husband, Jason Rudd.

JASON. There's only one beautiful person round here.

(*Awkward.*)

MARINA. (*Rescuing the situation.*) I was just telling Mrs Bantry how I hoped it wouldn't be painful for her, seeing the changes we'd made to her home.

DOLLY. You really mustn't give it another thought. Once my husband passed away, this was far too large for me to live in alone. And it's not as if I would have been here much anyway. My children both have children of their own now and not a nanny in sight, and you know what it's like with babies –

JASON. Where's that damn butler? He was meant to be getting the tea –

(**JASON** *rings the bell.*)

DOLLY. Is it true you're making a new film?

MARINA. Yes, at Hellingforth Studios.

DOLLY. Oh, I am glad. I was afraid that you'd disappeared from the picturehouse for good.

MARINA. The truth is, there aren't many great roles when you're no longer a slip of a girl... But this picture, this part... I couldn't resist.

JASON. You're gonna be just great, honey.

MARINA. Jason has written the film himself. It's a beautiful story, all about Catherine of Aragon. It's really (*Moved.*) very moving indeed.

DOLLY. And you're playing Catherine? How splendid. Now, how did she end up? *Divorced, beheaded, died, divorced, beheaded, survived.* Oh yes, that's right. Those poor women. All that kerfuffle, just to have a son!

(**JASON** *rings the bell violently.* **ELLA ZIELINKSY** *appears.*)

ELLA. The party's about to start.

MARINA. Oh, but we were going to have a cup of English tea.

ELLA. I don't see any tea.

(**GIUSEPPE** *appears with tea and cake.*)

GIUSEPPE. Tea is served.

JASON. You're too late.

ELLA. We're about to start.

GIUSEPPE. I was letting it stew.

ELLA. You mean brew.

(*Unspoken tension.*)

MARINA. Dear Giuseppe has been at my side for years.

ELLA. (*To* **GIUSEPPE**.) Aren't you meant to be serving the cocktails?

MARINA. (*To* **GIUSEPPE**.) Thank you, darling.

(*Beat.* **GIUSEPPE** *goes.*)

Our secretary, dearest Ella, oversaw all the work to the house. I do hope you don't mind but we've put in a few new bathrooms –

ELLA. Yeah, real fun it was too. The plumbing in this goddamn country –

DOLLY. (*Breaking off.*) They can be terribly coarse, Americans. Oh, did I tell you? They've put in six more bathrooms! Now, I've never understood the shower myself. How do you stop your hair from getting wet?

MISS MARPLE. Go back a bit. You were talking about your grandchildren and Mr Rudd said –

JASON. Where's that damn butler? He was meant to be getting the tea –

(**JASON** *rings the bell.*)

MISS MARPLE. And the same again, when you mentioned Henry the Eighth wanting a son...

(**ELLA**, **JASON** *and* **MARINA** *disappear.*)

Do they have any children?

DOLLY. I don't think so, but I do know Miss Gregg adopted two girls. They only stayed a few years. Then she sent them away.

MISS MARPLE. Oh bother!

DOLLY. What?

MISS MARPLE. I've dropped a stitch.

Those poor girls. I wonder why she sent them away.

DOLLY. Apparently she had a nervous breakdown. Twelve years ago. Hasn't made a film since. I read it in *Woman's Own*. At the hairdresser.

(**MISS MARPLE** *amused.*)

(*Defensively.*) It's very important to keep up with the modern world. We can't just sit in a chair and knit ourselves to death!

MISS MARPLE. I can't even seem to do that.

Knitting is like memory. It depends on your mood. And age.

DOLLY. Well, you've always been better at *unravelling* anyway. Unlike your friend, PC Plod.

(**CRADDOCK** *reacts, giving himself away.* **DOLLY** *gestures – I think he's still out there!*)

MISS MARPLE. (*Amused, playing ignorant.*) Oh, did I tell you? Dermot's been made a Chief Inspector now.

DOLLY. Really?!!

MISS MARPLE. *(Loudly.)* His mother would have been so proud. As am I, of course. We never get to say these things to people... What is it that stops us?

DOLLY. Common sense.

MISS MARPLE. Yes, but you're forgetting. I often looked after Dermot when his mother died. He was so unsettled by it all, poor chap... It's impossible to be cross with someone if you've had to change their short trousers a hundred times.

>   (**CRADDOCK** *indignant. He quickly opens and then closes the front door, as if re-entering. Reappears.*)

You're back.

CRADDOCK. It occurred to me that rather than waste time by tracking her down later, I should interview Mrs Bantry properly now, while she's here.

DOLLY. Kill two birds with one stone.

MISS MARPLE. Dolly's just been telling me about the secretary. Miss Ella...

CRADDOCK. Zielinsky. Polish descent.

>   (**MISS MARPLE** *raises an eyebrow.* **ELLA** *walks past, muttering in Polish.*)

I simply meant...

DOLLY. The secretary and the butler do not get on. I presume you gathered that?

CRADDOCK. I gathered a great deal from her, actually.

>   (**ELLA** *paces.*)

ELLA. To go and get herself murdered here! So inconvenient for us.

CRADDOCK. More inconvenient for the victim.

ELLA. What does she know? She's dead.

Jason told me they were going for Marina. Right?

CRADDOCK. Is Miss Gregg an easy woman to work for?

ELLA. She's a dream.

CRADDOCK. Really?

ELLA. *(Gives him a look.)* What do you think? The stories I could tell you... But she's a great artist. So you're made to feel it's a privilege to work with her. Actually, *(Sneezes.)* it's hell.

> (**ELLA** *takes out her atomiser [inhaler]. Inhales.*)

CRADDOCK. If you don't like her, why choose to work for her?

ELLA. Some days, I think I could just walk out that door. Never have to see her again.

CRADDOCK. Why don't you?

ELLA. I...I work for Jason.

So. You worked out "whodunnit"?

CRADDOCK. Is there anyone she suspects?

ELLA. I'm just the secretary. Why would she confide in me?

> (**ELLA** *disappears.*)

MISS MARPLE. Now, that is interesting...

CRADDOCK. Not particularly keen on Miss Gregg.

> (**MISS MARPLE**, *surprised, goes to speak. Doesn't.*)

Mrs Bantry... *(Pretending he doesn't already know.)* Did you happen to notice if Heather Leigh handed her drink to Marina Gregg at any point?

(**CHERRY** *appears, a little too quickly.*)

CHERRY. D'you want a top up? That must be stone cold by now.

MISS MARPLE. That would be lovely, thank you. Oh, perhaps you might be able to help us. Cherry was at the party too.

DOLLY. Were you?

Oh, you were the canapé girl!

CRADDOCK. You're Miss Baker? So, you were there yesterday.

CHERRY. That doesn't mean I did it.

MISS MARPLE. No one's saying you did. We're just trying to work out exactly what happened.

CRADDOCK. Well. I'm conducting an investigation.

(*Beat.*)

Miss Baker. Did you see Miss Gregg hand Heather Leigh a drink?

DOLLY. As I was about to tell you –

CHERRY. Yeah. Someone sneezed and she spilled her drink all down her dress. So Miss Gregg gave Heather Leigh her drink instead.

CRADDOCK. Mrs Bantry, does that corroborate with what you saw?

DOLLY. As it happens, yes.

(*Beat.*)

CRADDOCK. Did Miss Gregg pick out her drink herself or did someone hand it to her?

DOLLY. Oh. Er –

CHERRY. She got it from Giuseppe, I think his name is. The butler.

(We see everything reconstructed, as described.)

*(***GIUSEPPE*** appears, holding a tray of drinks.* ***MARINA*** *goes to him. They laugh at something together.* ***MARINA*** *very clearly picks her own drink.)*

MISS MARPLE. She definitely chose it herself?

*(***DOLLY*** *nods.)*

Who did you see approaching Miss Gregg between the time of Miss Gregg picking her drink and Heather Leigh drinking it?

CHERRY. I'd been told to stand in the corner with me tray and look "unobtrusive". *(Looks down.)*

MISS MARPLE. Did you see the feet of anyone going near Miss Gregg?

CHERRY. Well, yeah, but –

DOLLY. Heather Leigh marched over to Miss Gregg and started some dull-as-death story –

*(***HEATHER*** *far too close to* ***MARINA****.* ***JASON*** *joins them.)*

HEATHER. – when I heard that you were coming over to do *Antony and Cleopatra*! Oh, I was mad with excitement and then on the very day of the opening night, I went down with a rotten head cold. But I wasn't going to be beaten, so I put on a lot of make-up and stood in line for hours and you came right up to me and gave me your autograph, as if I mattered more than anyone. Oh, it was the happiest day of my life.

(A look of frozen horror on ***MARINA****'s face. She quickly puts back on a smile.)*

MARINA. How kind of you, to go to so much trouble.

CRADDOCK. And that's when the drink was spilled.

DOLLY. *(Simultaneously.)* No.

CHERRY. *(Simultaneously.)* Yes.

(Beat.)

DOLLY. Don't you remember? That was when Lola Brewster arrived.

*(**LOLA** appears.)*

HEATHER. Sorry, I don't mean to prattle on, it's just it meant such a lot to me.

MARINA. I'm so glad. Now, do excuse me. I really must say hi to my co-star.

*(**MARINA** goes to **LOLA**.)*

MISS MARPLE. Lola Brewster?

DOLLY. Oh Jane, don't tell me you haven't heard of her. She's been in all those films with those angry young men.

CRADDOCK. What did they say to each other?

DOLLY. I didn't catch it, but it didn't exactly look as if they were the best of friends.

*(**CRADDOCK** turns to **CHERRY**.)*

CHERRY. I was in me corner.

MISS MARPLE. *(To **CRADDOCK**.)* Have you spoken to Miss Brewster?

CRADDOCK. I wanted to talk to you first.

DOLLY. To get the gossip?

(Touché.)

I had a little chat with Lola, actually, at the party –

CRADDOCK. I'm sure you did –

MISS MARPLE. What did you make of her?

DOLLY. She was a dear.

LOLA. *(Goes to* **DOLLY.***)* Hi. I'm Lola. And you are…?

DOLLY. Dolly Bantry. I'm no one important, except I used to own this place.

LOLA. We're all important to ourselves. *(Smiles.)* You're one up on me, anyway. I wasn't actually invited.

DOLLY. Aren't you making a film with Miss Gregg?

LOLA. Sure, but she seems to have no idea who I am.

DOLLY. Who are you playing?

LOLA. Anne Boleyn.

DOLLY. Oh! The next wife!

>   *(Beat.)*

If you don't mind my asking, why did you come, if you weren't invited?

(Conspiratorial.) I came to look at the bathrooms.

LOLA. I thought it might be good to meet Marina away from the pressure of the set. Actually, *(Equally conspiratorial.)* I'm terrified. I've never worked with anyone famous before.

DOLLY. But aren't you famous, dear?

LOLA. Not like Marina. Mind you, no one's famous like Marina.

>   *(***LOLA** *disappears.)*

MISS MARPLE. Why go to a party when you haven't been invited?

CRADDOCK. Can we concentrate on the events?

MISS MARPLE. We all experience events differently.

CRADDOCK. Going back to what happened...

DOLLY. Well... *(To* **CHERRY**.*)* You started to go over to Miss Gregg, with your tray... But then you stopped...?

CHERRY. I was gonna offer her a vol-au-vent. But I lost my nerve.

CRADDOCK. Why?

CHERRY. She's ruddy famous.

CRADDOCK. Then what happened?

CHERRY. Miss Gregg went to talk to her secretary, but then you... *(To* **DOLLY**.*)* – sorry, I didn't catch your name.

DOLLY. Mrs Bantry. I used to own Gossington Hall.

CHERRY. Right. Well, you collared her. Something about –

DOLLY. I'd hardly say collared –

CHERRY. Toilets.

DOLLY. I went to congratulate Miss Gregg on her bathrooms.

CHERRY. Marina carried on to Miss wotshername.

DOLLY. Zielinsky.

(Beat.)

Miss Zielinsky put Miss Gregg's necklace straight.

CHERRY. Marina went back to that woman. Heather Leigh.

DOLLY. And then –

CHERRY. *(To* **DOLLY**.*)* Are you telling this story or am I?

MISS MARPLE. You're both doing very well.

CHERRY & DOLLY. Ta / Thank you.

(Beat.)

CRADDOCK. And then?

CHERRY. Miss Zielinsky sneezed –

> (**MARINA** *and* **HEATHER** *are conversing happily.* **JASON** *nearby.* **ELLA** *sneezes.*)

(*Quickly.*) And she spilled her drink all over her dress...

> (*We see* **HEATHER** *spill her drink over* **MARINA**'s *dress.*)

DOLLY. Heather Leigh looked mortified. Marina was doing everything she could to make Mrs Leigh feel better about the whole thing...

CHERRY. She was so nice about it too.

> (**MARINA** *graciously hands her drink to* **HEATHER**.)

DOLLY. And Heather Leigh knocked it back like a common bricklayer!

> (**HEATHER** *raises the glass to her lips. In the present day,* **CHERRY** *cries out.*)

CHERRY. One moment, she was chattering away, and then... I mean, I know people die and all that, but it was so...you know?

MISS MARPLE. (*Gently.*) Is that what you wanted to tell me, earlier?

> (*Beat.* **CHERRY** *looks down. Nods, quickly.*)

DOLLY. (*To* **CRADDOCK**.) So, who poisoned the drink?

CRADDOCK. My investigation is confidential.

DOLLY. You mean, you haven't a clue.

CRADDOCK. Thank you. You've been most helpful –

MISS MARPLE. You told me to ask about Tennyson.

DOLLY. Oh. Yes. It was after that tedious story –

(We see, replayed:)

HEATHER. And you gave me your autograph, as if I mattered more than anyone! Oh, it was the happiest day of my life.

(Music.* The sound of a mirror shattering. We can see the look of frozen horror on **MARINA**'s *face.)*

DOLLY. "The mirror crack'd from side to side;

'The doom is come upon me,' cried

The Lady of Shalott."

MISS MARPLE. You mean curse.

DOLLY. I beg your pardon?

MISS MARPLE. Curse. Not doom.

DOLLY. Oh. I prefer doom.

CRADDOCK. I don't think this is the time for a poetry discussion –

DOLLY. The point is, *if* you're interested, Heather Leigh was babbling on, and Miss Gregg's eyes began to wander – well, who can blame her – and then suddenly, on Miss Gregg's face there was a look of absolute terror.

CRADDOCK. Who was she looking at?

DOLLY. I don't know. I was looking at her.

CRADDOCK. She must have caught sight of someone. Who did she see?

DOLLY. *(Exasperated.)* I just told you…

---

* A license to produce *The Mirror Crack'd* does not include a performance license for any third-party or copyrighted recordings. Licensees should create their own.

MISS MARPLE. If she was frightened of someone, Dolly dear, it could be rather important.

DOLLY. I can't force myself to remember something I didn't see!

CRADDOCK. Miss Baker?

CHERRY. I didn't see nothing.

DOLLY. Anything.

CHERRY. That's right. I didn't see nothing.

(**DOLLY** *groans.*)

Right. Well, if you're done, I'd better start on lunch. Got a lovely bit of ham.

(**CHERRY** *turns to go.*)

CRADDOCK. Why were you helping at the party? I thought your job was to look after Miss Marple?

CHERRY. I saw this sign, saying they were looking for a girl, and I thought – I mean, you would, wouldn't you? Want to be in the same room as film stars…

CRADDOCK. You left an elderly lady to fend for herself?

MISS MARPLE. It was the "elderly lady" who insisted.

It's no good for Cherry to be stuck here all the time.

CRADDOCK. Just one more question, Miss Baker. Had you ever met Miss Gregg before?

CHERRY. I'm from Croydon.

(**CHERRY** *goes.*)

MISS MARPLE. I know what you're thinking but I'd be very surprised if Cherry had anything to do with it.

CRADDOCK. You said she's only been here a week. What do you know of her background?

MISS MARPLE. I know people. And I'm certain that Cherry could never hurt a fly.

CRADDOCK. Certainty without proof is no certainty at all.

(Beat.)

Well, I'd better head back to –

MISS MARPLE. Have you tested / every drink –

CRADDOCK. / Every drink was tested last night. Only that glass showed traces of the drug.

MISS MARPLE. So, someone in the room must have slipped the drug into the glass between the point of Miss Gregg picking it and Heather Leigh drinking it. Dolly, who was present in the room then?

DOLLY. The butler.

*(**GIUSEPPE** appears.)*

The husband.

*(**JASON** appears. Lines up beside **GIUSEPPE**.)*

The secretary.

*(**ELLA** appears, sneezes. Joins the line-up.)*

CRADDOCK. The co-star.

*(**LOLA** appears. Joins the line-up.)*

DOLLY. And your girl.

*(**CHERRY** appears. Joins the line-up.)*

MISS MARPLE. You're forgetting Mr Leigh.

*(**CYRIL** appears. Goes to join the line-up.)*

DOLLY. Oh. But it seems highly unlikely that he'd have anything to do with Miss Gregg…

(**CYRIL** *resignedly turns to go. Mr Invisible.*)

MISS MARPLE. One should never rule out anyone, no matter how absurd the possibility.

(**CYRIL** *goes back to join the line-up. The others shuffle up to make space for him.*)

(*Now all six potential suspects, standing in a line.*)

Which would mean that there are six people who could have had both the opportunity and a motive to slip the drug into Miss Gregg's drink.

CRADDOCK. I make it seven.

(**DOLLY** *stands up, to examine the line-up.*)

DOLLY. I can only see six...

(**DOLLY** *has inadvertently taken her place in the line up.*)

Oh!

MISS MARPLE. You can't possibly suspect Dolly.

CRADDOCK. "One should never rule out anyone, no matter how absurd the possibility."

(*The suspects disappear. Only* **DOLLY** *remains.*)

Why did you sell Gossington Hall?

DOLLY. As Jane will corroborate, it was perfectly dreadful living in that huge old mansion once Arthur died. I was thrilled that Miss Gregg wanted to buy it.

CRADDOCK. But you were in the room. Seeing someone else presiding over your old way of life –

MISS MARPLE. If we can just work out whom Miss Gregg was looking at, then we might discover which of these people it is that frightens her.

MISS MARPLE. Of course, you could just ask Miss Gregg.

DOLLY. You can't put that poor woman in a room with *him*! You'd never get a thing out of her.

> *(A ring at the doorbell.)*
>
> *(Awkward silence.)*
>
> *(***CHERRY*** appears with* ***CYRIL LEIGH.****)*

CHERRY. Mr Leigh.

MISS MARPLE. Thank you, Cherry. *(Beat.)* Oh, Mr Leigh, I was so sorry to hear about your poor wife.

CYRIL. Thank you. Excuse me for barging in like this, Miss Marple. The sergeant told me the Chief Inspector might be here.

CRADDOCK. Mr Leigh. I'm Chief Inspector Craddock.

CYRIL. … *(Trying to hold back his emotion.)* I thought, perhaps you'd want to talk to me.

CRADDOCK. Right. How are you, er, bearing up?

> *(The telephone rings.* ***CHERRY*** *goes to answer it. Everyone listens in.)*

CHERRY. St. Mary Mead 395?

Oh, hello.

I'm…Cherry. The help.

Yes, he's here… D'you want him?

All right. 'Ang on.

(To ***CRADDOCK.****)* She wants to speak to you.

It's Marina Gregg.

CRADDOCK. *(To* ***CYRIL.****)* I'm terribly sorry. Do excuse me.

CYRIL. But I have to tell you –

CRADDOCK. *(Into the telephone.)* Miss Gregg! How are you?

Yes, of course… Of course.

At the studio? Yes. Yes, I'll come right away.

> *(A flurry of activity.* **DOLLY** *helps* **MISS MARPLE** *onto her crutches;* **MISS MARPLE** *sets off,* **CRADDOCK** *chasing after her.)*

> *(Only* **CYRIL** *and* **CHERRY** *remain.* **CHERRY** *looks at* **CYRIL**. *Beat. Then* **CHERRY** *too quickly leaves.* **CYRIL** *sighs. Goes.)*

Scene Two

(Mid-morning. The film studios. As the film studios set up, **MISS MARPLE** *and* **CRADDOCK** *enter.* **MISS MARPLE**, *on crutches, picks up a film magazine, as she takes a seat.)*

MISS MARPLE. I imagine a man might feel cowed in the presence of a star, particularly a woman of such beauty –

CRADDOCK. She must be over fifty by now!

MISS MARPLE. Meaning?

(Beat.)

CRADDOCK. I can't believe I let you talk me into bringing you with me.

Remember, if anyone asks, you're my Aunt Jane and –

*(**LOLA** comes rushing in. Frantic.)*

LOLA. Did you see anyone come by?

CRADDOCK. I beg your pardon?

LOLA. Did you see anyone? With a handbag?

CRADDOCK. I'm afraid not but –

LOLA. Oh God!

CRADDOCK. All right, Miss. Calm down. I'm from the police –

LOLA. What?

CRADDOCK. You're perfectly safe. *(Shows his badge.)* Now, tell me what's happened.

LOLA. I... I'm sure it's nothing.

CRADDOCK. Someone took your handbag?

(Beat.)

LOLA. Yes...but it had nothing of value in it.

MISS MARPLE. So why are you so upset?

LOLA. I – I had a few personal things, of – sentimental value. That's all.

CRADDOCK. Where was the bag?

LOLA. Perhaps I left it at my hotel! I'd forget my own head if it wasn't –

*(**MARINA** appears.)*

MARINA. I am so sorry I kept you waiting – *(Sees **LOLA**.)* Oh. I hope I'm not interrupting...

CRADDOCK. Not at all. *(To **LOLA**.)* Perhaps I could have a word later, Miss Brewster? It is Miss Brewster, isn't it?

LOLA. I'm filming all day.

CRADDOCK. I will need to interview you. If you could telephone the local police station when you've finished, they can tell you where I am.

LOLA. *(Lightly.)* Of course.

*(**LOLA** turns to go.)*

MISS MARPLE. Miss Brewster? Where did you grow up?

LOLA. Los Angeles.

MISS MARPLE. Don't you call it a purse?

LOLA. *(Slightest hesitation; then smiles.)* When in England...

*(Odd moment. **LOLA** goes.)*

MARINA. We'll have more privacy in my dressing room. Please.

*(**MARINA** leads **CRADDOCK** into her dressing room. **MISS MARPLE** follows, on her crutches.)*

(**JASON** *is waiting in the dressing room.*)

JASON. Who's the dame?

CRADDOCK. My elderly aunt. She won't disturb us.

> (**CRADDOCK** *helps* **MISS MARPLE** *to sit down, out of the way, in the corner.*)

MARINA. How dear.

> (**MARINA** *waves graciously at* **MISS MARPLE**. **MISS MARPLE** *waves back.*)

CRADDOCK. Miss Gregg. I had a few private questions for you, if I may...

> (**CRADDOCK** *looks pointedly at* **JASON**. **JASON** *does not take the hint.*)

MARINA. Can't Jason stay?

CRADDOCK. If it were down to me, of course...but I'm afraid it's procedure...

JASON. Your aunt. Is that procedure too?

MISS MARPLE. I'm so sorry. I didn't mean to intrude... I don't get many outings these days.

CRADDOCK. I can have her removed, if it's a problem.

MARINA. I don't mind her being here.

MISS MARPLE. Thank you, dear. I won't say another word.

CRADDOCK. She really won't.

> (**CRADDOCK** *turns his back on* **MISS MARPLE**.)

JASON. Are you sure you're up to this, honey?

MARINA. Yes. I'm sure.

JASON. If you need me, I'll be right next door.

MARINA. Jason... I love you.

*(**JASON** kisses **MARINA**, shoots **CRADDOCK** another look. Goes.)*

It was nothing to do with Jason.

CRADDOCK. It really is police procedure.

MARINA. Sorry. I'm just so...

CRADDOCK. It must be horrible for you. Your new home.

MARINA. You're very sweet to understand.

What was it you wanted to ask me?

*(**CRADDOCK** crosses one leg over the other. Clears his throat. Tries to focus.)*

CRADDOCK. Miss Gregg... Is there any particular reason this tragedy has unsettled you so?

MARINA. It was my glass, wasn't it?

CRADDOCK. If you are in any danger, then my men and I will protect you. But I'll need you to answer a few questions, I'm afraid.

MARINA. Thank you, Inspector.

CRADDOCK. *(Smoothly.)* Chief Inspector, actually.

Did you pick out your own drink?

MARINA. Yes. Why? Oh.

CRADDOCK. So, your butler didn't direct you towards a particular drink?

MARINA. No.

CRADDOCK. Are you absolutely certain?

MARINA. Yes, I'm certain! You see... Look, if you're to know the truth...sometimes, I can be something of a beast. I don't mean to be but...

*(**GIUSEPPE** appears with his tray of drinks.)*

GIUSEPPE. You okay?

MARINA. All these ghastly people I've never met, who think they know me –

GIUSEPPE. The only way is to drink through the pain. What'll it be, Madam?

MARINA. What have you got, Sir?

GIUSEPPE. A strawberry daiquiri, or a strawberry daiquiri, or a strawberry daiquiri.

MARINA. I think I'll have a…strawberry daiquiri.

> (**GIUSEPPE** *indicates that the choice is hers! She chooses one at random.*)

I do try to be gracious but…

CRADDOCK. Everyone struggles with – obligations.

> (*He catches* **MISS MARPLE**'s *eye.*)

So, you chose a drink and then…

MARINA. Mrs Leigh came to talk to me, so I set my glass down –

CRADDOCK. Before you'd taken a sip?

MARINA. I never touched it. You see –

> (**HEATHER** *goes to* **MARINA**. **JASON** *joins them.*)

HEATHER. Oh Miss Gregg, do you remember me?

MARINA. I meet so many dear people… (*Puts her glass down.*)

HEATHER. (*Getting closer and closer to* **MARINA**.) Well, it was a few years ago now. I was mad with excitement, when I heard that you were coming over to play Cleopatra, and then on the very day of the opening, I went down with influenza! But I wasn't going to be beaten. I put on my best dress and I stood in line for hours and hours and hours, and you were so lovely to me, when it was my turn for your autograph. Oh, it was the happiest day of my life.

MARINA. How kind of you to go to so much trouble. You're here today because…

HEATHER. *(Annoyed.)* I'm Chair of St John Ambulance.

MARINA. That's just wonderful, Mrs…

HEATHER. Leigh. Heather Leigh.

> (**LOLA** *appears.*)

(Slightly abrasive.) Sorry, I don't mean to prattle on, it's just it meant such a lot to me.

MARINA. I'm so glad. Now, do excuse me. I really must say hi to my co-star.

HEATHER. But you will come back, won't you?

> (**MARINA** *turns back to the present.*)

MARINA. I didn't mean to be unkind but it can be very difficult, dealing with fans…

CRADDOCK. How long did you leave your drink there?

MARINA. Just a minute or two. I greeted Lola, and then went back to rescue Jason.

> (**MARINA** *goes to* **JASON**, *who is with* **HEATHER**.)

JASON. *(Whispers to* **MARINA**.*)* The second it's getting too much for you, just nod and I'll wrap things up –

CRADDOCK. Is he always so…

MARINA. My husband would never do anything to hurt me.

> (**JASON** *goes.*)

CRADDOCK. Did your butler come over to you at any point between you picking your drink and Mrs Leigh drinking it?

(**GIUSEPPE** *brings* **MARINA** *a couple of canapés on a plate.*)

GIUSEPPE. *(Warmly.)* Smoked salmon with cream cheese and a dash of lemon. No pepper. Not even a sniff.

MARINA. Giuseppe has been with me for seventeen years.

CRADDOCK. He said nineteen.

(**GIUSEPPE** *goes.*)

And Miss Zielinksy?

(**ELLA** *goes to* **MARINA**, *with her clipboard.*)

ELLA. After the party, you'll be meeting the Vicar, the head of the Women's Institute and – oh, your necklace...

(**ELLA** *lovingly readjusts* **MARINA***'s necklace.*)

MARINA. Ella is devoted to me.

(**ELLA** *goes.*)

CRADDOCK. What about Mrs Bantry?

MARINA. Who?

CRADDOCK. The woman who sold you Gossington Hall. A home that meant a great deal to her.

(**DOLLY** *steps forward.*)

DOLLY. You know what it's like with children, and grandchildren...

MARINA. Oh yes. A charming lady.

(**DOLLY** *smiles.*)

But that's ridiculous – I'd only just met her!

(**DOLLY** and **MISS MARPLE** share a gratified look. **DOLLY** leaves, head held high.)

CRADDOCK. Mr Leigh?

(**CYRIL** steps forward, goes to speak.)

MARINA. I didn't really... [notice him]

CRADDOCK. Yes.

(**CYRIL** sighs, goes.)

Did you go anywhere near the waitress?

(**CHERRY** appears.)

MARINA. There was a waitress?

(**CHERRY** goes.)

CRADDOCK. Did you go near or speak to anyone else during that time?

MARINA. No. Yes. Only Lola Brewster, as I said, but I barely know her –

LOLA. Hi. Do you remember me?

MARINA. Of course I do, sweetie. I saw you at the readthrough.

It's... Lola, right?

LOLA. – Right. God, your house, it's so...creaky.

MARINA. I'm sorry, I don't recall actually inviting you...

LOLA. You didn't. I wanted to say hi away from the filming, seeing as we're going to be together all the time.

MARINA. Sure. Well, you've said it now.

LOLA. Oh Marina, I've been watching your work since I was a little girl. I love old movies. Can we be friends?

MARINA. I don't have any friends.

(Beat. **LOLA** *leaves.)*

I shouldn't have been so cutting but these girls, they make you feel so...

CRADDOCK. Can you think of any reason why she might wish to harm you?

MARINA. I suppose there might be some envy on her part... But I should be envious of her! I mean, look at me... All the lotions and potions in the world can't hold back the force of time... *(To* **MISS MARPLE**.*)* Oh, God, I'm so sorry...

MISS MARPLE. We all find it so difficult to be the age we really are.

MARINA. I just meant, soon, Lola will be the star and I'll be the actress whose name you can't quite remember.

CRADDOCK. I'm sure no one could ever forget you.

MARINA. You're very kind, Chief Inspector...

CRADDOCK. Craddock. Scotland Yard.

MARINA. I don't envy Lola. Not really. When you're starting out, it's all you dream of, having your pictures shown in movie theatres all round the world, being noticed, wherever you go. You imagine it will make you happy.

CRADDOCK. Doesn't it?

MARINA. I thought it would. Everyone wants to be your friend. But because you're famous. Not because you're *you*.

MISS MARPLE. Is that why you don't have any friends?

CRADDOCK. *(Taking charge again.)* Do you take di-ethy... *(Clears throat.)* Calmo?

MARINA. We all do.

CRADDOCK. Americans?

MARINA. Actors.

CRADDOCK. Do you choose to take it yourself, or does your husband give it to you?

MARINA. I choose to take it. Why?

CRADDOCK. Does Mr Rudd have his own supply?

MARINA. *Our* supply is in the cabinet in our ensuite, but Jason only ever gives it to me when I ask.

CRADDOCK. As far as you know.

MARINA. No. I'd know.

CRADDOCK. You're sure about that?

MARINA. Yes!

> *(Beat.)*

CRADDOCK. Forgive me. I just need to get everything clear. For –

MARINA. *(Smiles.)* Procedure?

CRADDOCK. Exactly. Now. How did Heather Leigh end up with your drink?

MARINA. It was one of those stupid things. Someone sneezed –

> *(**ELLA** appears, sneezes.)*

Ella, I expect, she gets this terrible hayfever –

> *(**ELLA** sneezes. Fumbles for her atomiser.)*

> *(**HEATHER**, startled, has spilled her drink over Marina's dress. Mortified, **HEATHER** dabs at **MARINA**'s dress with her handkerchief.)*

HEATHER. I'm so sorry! Your poor dress –

MARINA. Please, don't give it another thought. *(Conspiratorially.)* I hate this dress, but it was a present from Jason, and yah-di-yah-da –

HEATHER. You're just saying that –

MARINA. No, really, you've done me quite the favour! Now, what were you drinking?

HEATHER. A strawberry wotsit… Just like you.

MARINA. *(Kindly.)* Well, why don't you have this one and –

HEATHER. You'd let me have your drink?! You really are just as lovely as I remembered.

> (**MARINA** *picks up her drink, hands it to* **HEATHER.** **HEATHER** *goes to drink.* **MARINA** *can't bear it.*)

MARINA. It was my fault –

CRADDOCK. No. Miss Gregg. You behaved impeccably. You mustn't hold yourself responsible in any way.

> *(A moment.* **MARINA** *produces a knife and a torn picture of herself, ripped from a magazine.)*

MARINA. I found this today, in my dressing room. The knife had been stabbed right through my eyes.

CRADDOCK. Where is this picture of you from?

MARINA. It could be any magazine. *Tatler*, *Vogue* –

CRADDOCK. I meant, you hadn't given this picture to anyone?

MARINA. No. I expect someone meant to frighten me but really, it just made me terribly angry, which is why I called you.

*(**CRADDOCK** takes the knife with his handkerchief, carefully bags the knife and stabbed picture.)*

CRADDOCK. You have no idea who put this there.

MARINA. No! I don't understand.

CRADDOCK. If I may… You're a very beautiful woman, Miss Gregg –

*(**MISS MARPLE** reacts.)*

MARINA. That's just luck, isn't it? The face you're given.

When I look in the mirror now, I want to smash it to pieces. Perhaps that seems crazy *(Looks to **MISS MARPLE**.)* if you had nothing to lose…

MISS MARPLE. We all had something to lose.

CRADDOCK. The point is, I expect many men have fallen in love with you. Women envy you –

MARINA. You're saying it could have been anyone.

CRADDOCK. No, it has to be someone who was close to you that day at the party.

*(We see again: **JASON**, **ELLA**, **LOLA**, **DOLLY**, **CHERRY**, **GIUSEPPE**. **CYRIL** hovers, uncertain.)*

MARINA. People I barely know… Or the few people I can actually trust…

Maybe it was one of the catering team –

CRADDOCK. And you just happened to pick out the right drink?

*(**MARINA** thinks about it. Appalled. **GIUSEPPE**, meanwhile, appears in the background, eavesdropping.)*

Is there someone you suspect?

MARINA. No.

CRADDOCK. Are you sure? There's no one who frightens you?

MARINA. *(Shakes her head.)* I so wish I could help you.

CRADDOCK. Of course.

If you think of anything else, you know where to find me.

> (**CRADDOCK** *turns to go.*)

MISS MARPLE. *(Quietly.)* Dermot. Weren't you going to ask about the Tennyson?

CRADDOCK. I don't...

MISS MARPLE. I think it might be rather important.

CRADDOCK. *(Sighs.)* Apparently, while Heather Leigh was talking to you, you looked over her shoulder and you saw someone who seemed to alarm you.

MARINA. Alarm me? Who should have alarmed me?

MISS MARPLE. My dear, if there's someone you're protecting –

MARINA. Protecting? What d'you – Oh... I think I know what you mean.

CRADDOCK. Go on.

MARINA. The trouble is, I hear the same things over and over again, how someone once saw me outside a theatre, or on an airplane, and I have to pretend to remember. Mrs Leigh was telling me one of those stories and I'm afraid I stopped listening and then I realised that she'd finished and she was gazing at me and I hadn't the faintest idea what to say. I guess I just...froze.

CRADDOCK. So, you weren't frightened of someone?

> (**GIUSEPPE** *enters quickly.*)

GIUSEPPE. Mr Rudd needs you in costume.

MISS MARPLE. Are you Mr Renzo?

GIUSEPPE. Why?

MISS MARPLE. I toured Italy as a young lady with – a friend of mine. We had a lovely week in Naples.

GIUSEPPE. I've never been.

Marina… When you're ready…

> (**GIUSEPPE** *leaves.*)

MARINA. If you'll forgive me –

CRADDOCK. Of course.

> (**MISS MARPLE** *deliberately drops her film magazine as* **MARINA** *goes to leave.*)

MISS MARPLE. Oh, my dear…

> (**MARINA** *stops, picks up the magazine and hands it to* **MISS MARPLE**.)

I'm glad you've made a full recovery.

MARINA. I beg your pardon?

MISS MARPLE. Your comeback. It's been such a long time. I suppose that's the lot of the woman. Just as one is getting somewhere, one is interrupted by having children –

MARINA. I don't have any children.

MISS MARPLE. Neither do I. It's funny, isn't it, how the world makes you feel as if you've somehow failed, if you decided not to produce children.

CRADDOCK. That will be all. Thank you, Miss Gregg.

MARINA. No, it's not that. I did want children.

MISS MARPLE. Oh, I'm sorry. I didn't mean to... I too once had hopes of a family...

CRADDOCK. *(Uncomfortable.)* Jane –

MISS MARPLE. *(Indicating* **CRADDOCK**.*)* I looked after this poor chap on occasion but, well, time goes by...

MARINA. Yes. Time goes by.

> (**MARINA** *and* **MISS MARPLE** *both momentarily caught in their own thoughts, their own losses.*)

(Catching herself.) If you'll excuse me –

CRADDOCK. Of course.

MISS MARPLE. Could you not have children of your own?

MARINA. I'm sorry... *(To* **CRADDOCK**.*)* Who is this woman?

CRADDOCK. Nobody. Well, she's my aunt. Well, not really my aunt but –

MISS MARPLE. Dermot feels sorry for me because I've no family of my own. But you adopted, I believe...?

MARINA. It's common knowledge.

MISS MARPLE. So does that mean you couldn't have children of your own?

MARINA. ...

MISS MARPLE. And so you took in two girls...

MARINA. You've clearly been reading the gossip columns.

MISS MARPLE. But you sent the girls away.

MARINA. Is that what people think?

I became unwell.

MISS MARPLE. Was there anything in particular that triggered your illness?

MARINA. ...My work can be very demanding at times...

MISS MARPLE. Of course.

What were the girls like?

MARINA. I don't see...

MISS MARPLE. I'm sorry. I didn't mean to intrude. I suppose you don't really think about them now...

MARINA. Of course I think about them! Alice, she was really fun. Full of life. Charlotte was a sweet, sweet soul. The most loyal little kitten I ever met.

MISS MARPLE. I think it might be vital we find them now. Don't you think?

MARINA. It can't have been anything to do with them.

MISS MARPLE. Are you sure?

MARINA. ...Those girls loved me.

MISS MARPLE. Even though you sent them away?

MARINA. It wasn't like that. They didn't want to see me but [they'd never] –

MISS MARPLE. Because they felt...rejected?

MARINA. No!

MISS MARPLE. Then...ah. Replaced.

MARINA. ...

MISS MARPLE. You had a baby?

MARINA. I told you, I don't have children...

MISS MARPLE. No?

> (**CRADDOCK** *goes to speak.* **MISS MARPLE** *stops him.*)
>
> (*Silence.* **MARINA** *can't hold back the tears.*)

MISS MARPLE. Oh my dear. I'm very sorry.

What happened to your baby?

MARINA. ...The doctors told me he wasn't right in the head. My husband – at the time, his name was Peter – he thought it best if we kept it from the world, so no one would write nasty stories.

I tried to look after him, my baby, Sam, but... Then I, I wasn't very well, so Peter insisted we send the girls away. I wanted them to be happy. I thought it was the best thing for them.

Then Peter left us, and my poor boy, he was so...

They said it would be better to let him be in a place where he'd be cared for... I went to visit him, whenever I could, but... They didn't even let me take him home, at the very end.

MISS MARPLE. *(Gently.)* When did he die?

MARINA. Six months ago. That's why Jason brought us here. To start again.

MISS MARPLE. Who's they?

    (Silence.)

My dear... Who wouldn't let you take your child home?

    (**JASON** *comes in. Sees* **MARINA**'s *tear-stained face.*)

JASON. Is there a problem?

MARINA. No. No, I'm just –

JASON. *(To* **CRADDOCK**.*)* Inspector, I warned you –

CRADDOCK. *Chief* Inspector.

(To **MARINA**.*)* Is it your husband who frightens you?

(The below, overlapping:)

MARINA. No –

JASON. How dare you?

CRADDOCK. I can have him arrested –

JASON. You have no idea –

CRADDOCK. Questioned, at the police station –

JASON. Who the hell tried to kill her –

MARINA. That's enough –

JASON. You couldn't stop a murderer if he was standing right next to you!

CRADDOCK. You may well be a powerful man in your walk of life but I have to remind you that we are all equal in the eyes of the law –

MARINA. Jason –

JASON. Why don't you just come out and say it? You think I tried to kill my wife!

MARINA. Honey. I told them about Sam.

JASON. What? Why?

MARINA. They wanted to know why I had to send my girls away.

JASON. Oh, sweetheart.

*(**JASON** takes **MARINA**'s hand. He turns back to **CRADDOCK**.)*

If this gets out –

CRADDOCK. This is a confidential investigation –

JASON. I mean it. If either of you ever breathes a word –

CRADDOCK. Yes?

(Another stand off.)

MISS MARPLE. Miss Gregg. I can assure you we both understand that some things are too painful to be made public. This will go no further. Will it, Dermot?

CRADDOCK. You have my word.

MARINA. *(To* **CRADDOCK**.*)* Thank you. *(To* **MISS MARPLE**.*)* And thank you, Mrs...

MISS MARPLE. Miss. Jane Marple.

(The two women look at each other. A moment.)

JASON. Right then –

MARINA. Could I... Could I have a minute?

JASON. You heard her –

MARINA. Alone?

JASON. ...I'll be right outside.

*(***JASON*** kisses ***MARINA***. He turns to usher out ***MISS MARPLE*** and ***CRADDOCK***.)*

MARINA. Oh, Detective Craddock, why don't you stay and watch the filming?

*(***JASON*** leaves. ***CRADDOCK*** helps ***MISS MARPLE*** off. ***MARINA***, alone, stares at her face in the mirror in her dressing table. She cries.)*

*(Suddenly, a sound. ***MARINA*** startles, frightened.)*

Is someone there?

Scene Three

*(The film set. On crutches, **MISS MARPLE** makes her way determinedly towards a seat in the corner. **CRADDOCK** trying to block her way. A fierce but whispered confrontation:)*

CRADDOCK. Are you sure I can't telephone for a taxi cab for you?

MISS MARPLE. I shall keep out of everyone's way.

CRADDOCK. That's what you said earlier! But you were a bloody liability.

*(**JASON** oversees as company members become the members of the crew, setting up cameras, and mics.)*

MISS MARPLE. Liability? Dermot, you hadn't got a thing out of her!

CRADDOCK. Yes, well, I'm certain her private life has nothing to do with this!

MISS MARPLE. Certainty without proof is no certainty at all.

*(**MISS MARPLE** takes her seat. **ELLA** appears, with her clipboard.)*

It's very impressive that you're all carrying on, after what's just happened.

ELLA. Have you any idea how much it costs, to lose a day's – [filming] *(**ELLA** interrupts herself, sneezing.)*

MISS MARPLE. Bless you.

ELLA. Goddamn English flowers.

*(**ELLA** takes out her atomiser. Inhales.)*

(**MARINA** *joins the set.* **ELLA** *gazes at her. Everyone claps.* **MARINA** *acknowledges the applause, graciously.*)

MISS MARPLE. *(To* **ELLA**.*)* Miss Zielinsky, I presume? May I ask, what is this scene about?

ELLA. Catherine of Aragon has walked in on Henry in bed with Anne Boleyn, her lady-in-waiting. Catherine's called Anne in for a cat fight.

MISS MARPLE. That's very clear. Thank you, dear.

ASSISTANT DIRECTOR. Quiet, please. We're about to shoot.

JASON. Marina, sweetheart. Remember we had you in the chair?

MARINA. Of course.

(**MARINA** *discombobulated. She takes her seat.*)

JASON. Take all the time you need.

MARINA. I'm fine.

AD. Settle down, everyone. We're going for a take. Red light and bell.

(We see the red light, hear the bell.)

AD. Catherine of Aragon, scene twenty-one, take one. *(He/she claps.)*

And we are rolling.

JASON. And...action.

(**LOLA** *[as* **ANNE***] kneels before* **MARINA** *[as* **CATHERINE***].*)

MARINA/CATHERINE. *(Spanish accent.)* Why?

LOLA/ANNE. *(English accent.)* It was not – I did not –

MARINA/CATHERINE. *(Getting up.)* He forced himself upon you?

LOLA/ANNE. ...No.

MARINA/CATHERINE. I did not think it of you.

LOLA/ANNE. Madam, I will do anything –

MARINA/CATHERINE. Then go far from here.

LOLA/ANNE. Please –

MARINA/CATHERINE. I thought you loved me.

LOLA. ...

Sorry.

JASON. Still rolling. Give her the line, please.

AD. I beg you –

LOLA. Yes. Sorry.

(As **ANNE.***)* I beg you not to send me from your sight.

MARINA/CATHERINE. Mine or his? You know nothing of what it is to love.

LOLA/ANNE. ...

JASON. Cut.

AD. Cut! Save the red!

(We hear the bell; the red light goes off.)

JASON. What's wrong?

MARINA. She keeps drying, darling.

AD. It's: "I know the pain it causes."

LOLA. Yes. Sorry.

JASON. We'll go again.

AD. Quick as we can, please. Quiet, everyone. Red light and bell.

(We hear the bell, see the red light.)

AD. Catherine of Aragon, scene twenty-one, take two, pickup. *(He/she claps.)*

JASON. We'll pick up from your line, Lola, "I know the pain".

And...action.

LOLA/ANNE. I know the pain it causes.

True beauty, my lady, comes from inner grace, and that is what the world sees in you...

Sorry.

JASON. What's wrong now?

LOLA. D'you think she really believes all that?

JASON. Cut!

AD. Cut! Save the red.

(Bell, red light off.)

JASON. She believes it.

LOLA. I don't.

MARINA. You don't have to believe it, honey. You just have to say the lines.

LOLA. Your face has cracked.

MARINA. I beg your pardon?

LOLA. Your powder. There's a crack, just there – *(Pointing it out.)*

MARINA. Don't touch me.

JASON. Ladies, please! We'll take a break.

AD. That's five minutes, please. Don't wander off and keep the noise DOWN. We are going again in five minutes.

(**LOLA** *walks off.*)

MARINA. *(To* **GIUSEPPE**.*)* Sweetie, get me some water. It's boiling in here. Three cubes of ice –

GIUSEPPE. I know.

(**GIUSEPPE** *leaves.*)

ELLA. Here – *(Offers her own drink.)*

MARINA. Thank you.

JASON. *(To* **MARINA**.*)* I'd better check on Lola.

(**JASON** *leaves.*)

MARINA. Ella – go with him. Make sure Lola's okay.

(Beat. **ELLA** *leaves. The* **AD** *goes too.)*

(Getting up from her chair.) I'm sorry you had to witness that.

CRADDOCK. Is it normally so...

MARINA. No. She really doesn't like me, huh?

MISS MARPLE. I wouldn't say that. In fact –

(A studio lamp begins to wobble from above. They all hear the noise. **MARINA** *shrieks, jumps out of the way. The lamp comes crashing down, narrowly missing* **MARINA**.*)*

CRADDOCK. *(Urgent.)* How would someone get up there?

MARINA. I don't know. Maybe, that way? *(Indicates opposite direction from the one in which* **GIUSEPPE** *went.)*

(**CRADDOCK** *runs off.*)

I was standing right there!

MISS MARPLE. Don't you think it's time you told us the truth?

MARINA. I don't know what you mean.

MISS MARPLE. Who is it you're trying to protect?

MARINA. I already told you –

MISS MARPLE. No, Miss Gregg. I know there's someone you are afraid of, and if you don't tell us who, then you will almost certainly lose your life.

> *(They look at each other. Neither gives an inch.)*

ACT TWO

Scene One

*(**CRADDOCK** helps **MISS MARPLE** into her chair.)*

CRADDOCK. Bye then.

*(**CRADDOCK** starts to go.)*

MISS MARPLE. Could you… *(Indicates crutches.)*

*(**CRADDOCK** puts the crutches in reach. He turns, again, to go.)*

CRADDOCK. Cheerio.

MISS MARPLE. You musn't blame yourself.

CRADDOCK. *(Turning back.)* What? If you hadn't been so…

MISS MARPLE. Yes?

CRADDOCK. You haven't been trained to handle a witness!

MISS MARPLE. Handle? Isn't it rather about getting them to talk to you?

CRADDOCK. I should never have allowed you to –

MISS MARPLE. Speak?

CRADDOCK. It's a very delicate situation.

MISS MARPLE. How can no one have seen a thing?

CRADDOCK. Someone must have cut the cable.

MISS MARPLE. Well. They missed. So we still have a chance –

CRADDOCK. We?

They might have talked to me if you hadn't been there!

MISS MARPLE. You don't allow them any silences to fill!

CRADDOCK. You're a spinster, not a detective.

(Beat.)

MISS MARPLE. I'm sure she would have told me if you hadn't blundered back in.

CRADDOCK. Blundered?!

Told you what?

MISS MARPLE. Of whom she is afraid. It just doesn't make any sense, why she'd continue to risk her life to protect someone. Unless –

CRADDOCK. Not all that again.

MISS MARPLE. What other explanation is there?

CRADDOCK. Maybe, maybe she saw something which reminded her of... I don't know. You're the one who has read Proust.

MISS MARPLE. Go on.

CRADDOCK. Just an example, I was eating apple crumble when Father came in to tell me that my mother had died. Whenever I see apple crumble...

MISS MARPLE. You've never talked about her. Your mother.

CRADDOCK. I'm just saying, there might be another explanation. Something that reminded Miss Gregg of something else. Or perhaps she had a sudden toothache.

MISS MARPLE. You were so young.

(Beat.)

CRADDOCK. You think it matters. The son.

MISS MARPLE. To Miss Gregg? More than we can imagine. To the investigation, I don't know.

Mr Rudd seemed terribly anxious no one should find out.

CRADDOCK. I'm sure it was the best thing for the child.

MISS MARPLE. So, we lock up anyone who's a burden?

CRADDOCK. I simply meant, if Miss Gregg was unwell herself, it must have been a real strain for her, caring for a sick child –

MISS MARPLE. Who told her she was unwell?

CRADDOCK. What d'you mean?

MISS MARPLE. If someone you trust tells you you're not well, the easiest thing is to believe it.

When did Miss Gregg marry Mr Rudd?

*(**JASON** appears.)*

JASON. I have dedicated the last eight years to nursing her back to health.

MISS MARPLE. Eight years is a very long time to be with someone so...

CRADDOCK. What?

(Beat.)

MISS MARPLE. Don't these people insure their films?

*(The doorbell rings. **JASON** disappears. No one answers the door.)*

Where's Cherry?

CRADDOCK. *(Irritated.)* I'll go.

> (**CRADDOCK** *lets in* **CYRIL LEIGH**.)

Mr Leigh. I'm so sorry. I got caught up –

CYRIL. Yes. But I have to tell you –

> *(The doorbell goes again. Beat.)*

CRADDOCK. Excuse me.

> (**CRADDOCK** *goes off to answer it, muttering "It's like Piccadilly bloody Circus!"*)

> (**CRADDOCK** *lets in* **LOLA**.)

LOLA. Your sergeant told me to come here...?

CRADDOCK. Miss Brewster. Just a few questions, if I may?

CYRIL. Sorry. Could I just –

CRADDOCK. Do forgive me, Mr Leigh, but I'm afraid I really need to interview Miss Brewster. I'll call round later, all right?

CYRIL. But –

CRADDOCK. If you'll excuse me.

> *(Beat.* **CYRIL** *leaves, reluctantly.)*

MISS MARPLE. Perhaps, my dear, we could all do with a cup of tea. Dermot, could you put the kettle on?

LOLA. Oh yes please! If it's not too much trouble?

> (**CRADDOCK** *sighs, goes, muttering under his breath.)*

MISS MARPLE. Did you find your handbag?

LOLA. No, but I told you –

MISS MARPLE. You seemed so upset.

LOLA. I know it's stupid. Just sentimental reasons.

MISS MARPLE. Have you managed to come up with any yet?

LOLA. ...

MISS MARPLE. You see, unless you tell us what was in your bag, it looks very suspicious.

LOLA. But, he might think something that's not true.

MISS MARPLE. He's a very clever man. He'll see beyond appearances.

> (**CRADDOCK** *has returned.* **MISS MARPLE** *indicates he shouldn't speak. Eventually:*)

LOLA. *(To* **CRADDOCK**.*)* There was a knife. In my bag.

CRADDOCK. Why?

LOLA. My father gave it to me. Before he died.

CRADDOCK. Did you have it with you at Gossington?

LOLA. What? No!

CRADDOCK. But you took it with you to the studios.

LOLA. Look, I...

CRADDOCK. Yes?

LOLA. There's a murderer on the loose. I thought it might be a good idea to protect myself.

CRADDOCK. Is this your knife?

> (**CRADDOCK** *takes out an enlarged photograph of Lola's knife/takes out the knife carefully, with his handkerchief.*)

LOLA. Thank God! Where did you find it?

CRADDOCK. Miss Gregg's dressing room. Stabbed through a picture of Miss Gregg.

LOLA. God! But that was nothing to do with me! Someone stole my bag! Why would I bring it to your attention if I was gonna do something like that?

CRADDOCK. If Marina died, you would be the star of the picture.

LOLA. It would be called off. Jason's doing this for her... The way they all run after her.

MISS MARPLE. Miss Brewster, when did your father die?

LOLA. Last summer.

MISS MARPLE. It's wretched, losing a parent. You feel so alone in the world.

LOLA. Yes.

MISS MARPLE. Oh – which father are we talking about? Your own father or one of your adoptive fathers?

LOLA. I beg your pardon?

(**MISS MARPLE** *shows* **LOLA** *the film magazine she took from the studios.*)

MISS MARPLE. It says here that you were born in England. Whereabouts?

LOLA. I don't see –

MISS MARPLE. I expect you've wondered about her your whole life. The woman who took you from your home and then discarded you.

LOLA. ...How do you know?

MISS MARPLE. Why else would you mind all this so much?

(*Beat.*)

LOLA. I just wanted to see her again.

MISS MARPLE. Why haven't you told her who you really are?

LOLA. ...That first day, at the readthrough –

> (**MARINA** *appears.* **LOLA** *stares at her.* **LOLA** *goes to* **MARINA**. *Tentative; shy.*)

LOLA. Marina...?

MARINA. And you are?

LOLA. You don't remember me...?

MARINA. I'm afraid I meet so many dear people...

LOLA. You really don't remember me.

MARINA. Should I?

Oh yes. Weren't you in one of those gritty modern thrillers?

> (**MARINA** *disappears.*)

LOLA. Marina called herself my mother for five years. She didn't even recognise me.

MISS MARPLE. I imagine Miss Gregg sees so many people, she has stopped really looking.

And perhaps you have changed a great deal since then. I expect Giuseppe didn't recognize you either –

LOLA. I know, but –

MISS MARPLE. And you've changed your name.

LOLA. Yes. My name was Alice, but –

MISS MARPLE. So it's hardly surprising that Miss Gregg didn't recognise the little girl she gave up twelve years ago...

LOLA. ...I was so frightened that someone had taken the knife to hurt her, and it would all be my fault.

MISS MARPLE. Why did she adopt you?

LOLA. Why don't you ask her?

CRADDOCK. Miss Brewster –

LOLA. Look. She'd been trying for a baby for years. I guess she decided that we would have to do.

CRADDOCK. We?

LOLA. My little sister, Charlotte, came too. We had everything… Clothes and toys and a beautiful house… and "Mommy".

MISS MARPLE. I believe she cared for you very much.

LOLA. We should have stayed with our real mum. At least there was no pretence.

MISS MARPLE. Pretence?

LOLA. There were eight of us in a slum. Mum wrote to them all, all the movie stars, begging them to adopt her kids. Marina was the only one dumb enough to say yes. So Charlotte and I were packed off.

MISS MARPLE. *(Gently.)* It must have been very unsettling, losing a second mother.

LOLA. We're not allowed to…

CRADDOCK. My enquiry is confidential.

(**LOLA** *scratches intermittently at her arm.*)

LOLA. She fell pregnant. She had no need of us after that.

MISS MARPLE. I'm sure it was more complicated than that.

CRADDOCK. What happened to you?

LOLA. Paid off, and re-adopted. Made to swear never to say a word.

I wrote to her – for years. She never wrote back.

CRADDOCK. So, you're angry with her. The mother who discarded you –

LOLA. Okay! But I'd never have hurt her.

CRADDOCK. So why d'you really have a knife?

(*The kettle is now whistling loudly.*)

MISS MARPLE. The tea, Dermot?

(**CRADDOCK**, *deeply irritated, heads off again.*)

You put the milk in first.

CRADDOCK. I have made tea before.

(**CRADDOCK** *leaves.*)

MISS MARPLE. There's a little mark, there, on your dress –

(**MISS MARPLE** *points out a bloodstain on* **LOLA**'s *arm.*)

LOLA. Oh. Er…

MISS MARPLE. Have you hurt yourself?

LOLA. No, I… (*Hiding the bloodstain.*)

MISS MARPLE. Oh. Oh, my dear.

LOLA. Please… It's just a…

MISS MARPLE. You have suffered very much. You don't need to punish yourself further.

Have you ever considered that Miss Gregg simply wasn't allowed to see you?

LOLA. Marina does whatever she wants.

MISS MARPLE. Does she?

(*A moment. Broken by* **CRADDOCK** *re-appearing, holding cups of tea.*)

And where is Charlotte now?

LOLA. No idea. They sent us to different families… I haven't seen her since.

MISS MARPLE. Oh, my dear.

CRADDOCK. About this knife –

MISS MARPLE. *(Interrupting.)* Sorry. If I may. Just one more question. Did you see who Miss Gregg was looking at when she was talking to Mrs Leigh?

LOLA. No. But I know the moment you mean. It looked as if she'd seen a ghost.

MISS MARPLE. Do you have any idea who was in her eyeline?

LOLA. I'm really sorry. I was looking at *her*.

Can I go now?

MISS MARPLE. Of course.

CRADDOCK. But –

MISS MARPLE. Let her go.

(A moment.)

CRADDOCK. Don't go anywhere near Gossington Hall, or leave the village, without letting the police know.

*(**LOLA** turns to go.)*

MISS MARPLE. Alice?

LOLA. *(Smiles.)* No one's called me by real name for years.

MISS MARPLE. Talk to Marina. I believe it would mean the world to her, to find you.

*(**LOLA** goes. Beat.)*

How interesting.

CRADDOCK. Rejected daughter carries a knife around.

MISS MARPLE. She said it looked as if Marina had seen a *ghost…*

CRADDOCK. Lock the door when I've gone.

(**CRADDOCK** *turns to go again.*)

MISS MARPLE. Dermot. She, she uses the knife on herself.

CRADDOCK. I don't understand.

MISS MARPLE. Neither do I. Not really. The girl at the post office does it. A way of coping with despair, I suppose.

CRADDOCK. But that's obscene!

MISS MARPLE. No. Being abandoned not once but twice by a mother, *that's* obscene.

CRADDOCK. Goodbye, Aunt Jane.

(*The sound of the door.*)

MISS MARPLE. Ah, thank goodness. (*Calls.*) Cherry, dear, I was getting quite [worried] –

(**DOLLY** *bursts in.*)

Dolly!

DOLLY. Oh Jane, I thought you ought to know, this morning I saw your girl, *Cherry*, hurtling along, and then jumping on a *bus*! And then, just now, I saw her racing back, carrying great big baskets of shopping, towards you, or so I assumed, and then suddenly she stopped and sat down on the vicarage wall, looking for all the world like a common vagabond.

(**CHERRY** *has let herself in. Listens in, undetected.*)

MISS MARPLE. Now, where could Cherry be going, on a bus…?

Ah. But what could she have seen…?

(*The scene at the studio reappears.*)

Oh, how stupid of me.

CRADDOCK & DOLLY. What?

MISS MARPLE. At the studio today –

MARINA. Don't touch me!

(**LOLA** *goes.*)

JASON. Ladies, please!

MISS MARPLE. Miss Brewster went to her dressing room.

JASON. We'll take a break.

AD. That's five minutes, please. Don't wander off and keep the noise DOWN. We are going again in five minutes.

MISS MARPLE. Mr. Rudd went to make sure she was all right.

JASON. I'd better go check on Lola.

(**JASON** *goes.*)

MARINA. *(To* **GIUSEPPE**.*)* Sweetie, get me some water. It's boiling in here. Three cubes of ice –

GIUSEPPE. I know.

(**GIUSEPPE** *goes to leave.* **MISS MARPLE** *grabs his arm. Stops him from leaving.*)

ELLA. *(Handing over her drink.)* Here, have mine.

MARINA. Thank you.

MISS MARPLE. Miss Zielinsky followed.

MARINA. Ella, go with Jason. Make sure Lola's okay.

CRADDOCK. They all went the same way...

MISS MARPLE. Except Mr. Renzo.

(**MISS MARPLE** *releases* **GIUSEPPE**.*)*

He went to get some water. And moments later...

(The sound of the lamp falling.)

GIUSEPPE. Nineteen years, I follow her everywhere.

MISS MARPLE. All those years, he's had to put up with –

GIUSEPPE. *(Annoyed.)* Smoked salmon with cream cheese and a dash of lemon. No pepper. Not even a sniff.

MISS MARPLE. Why would one stay? Having to cater for every whim, anticipate every demand?

GIUSEPPE. Three cubes of ice; the faintest sliver of lime.

CRADDOCK. Some people know their place in the world.

GIUSEPPE. I love Marina. Love.

MISS MARPLE. Always on the outside, tolerated only because he was useful... That must have been very lonely indeed.

GIUSEPPE. I keep her safe, I keep her...clear.

MISS MARPLE. Clear...from what?

CRADDOCK. We've already been through that –

MISS MARPLE. He would have been there, when she had the baby. All these years, living with her secrets, and her demands –

CRADDOCK. So why not just leave?

MISS MARPLE. He knew too much. She wouldn't let him.

CRADDOCK. Surely all this begs the question, why now?

MISS MARPLE. Perhaps something happened, the final straw. Or perhaps he felt safe here. On a little island, the other side of the world...

CRADDOCK. But why would she protect him?

MISS MARPLE. Because she couldn't bear to lose him. Her devoted butler, always at her side. The only person who has ever been a constant.

MISS MARPLE. Perhaps he did recognise Miss Brewster. Maybe he went through her bag to confirm his suspicions and found the knife, so he used it to frighten Miss Gregg yet further.

DOLLY. Oh Jane, you are clever.

CRADDOCK. I told you there was something about him…

MISS MARPLE. You said he was Italian.

None of this means it necessarily was him. No, I don't think we can do anything until we have talked to Cherry.

> (**CHERRY** *comes in, carrying baskets of shopping.*)

Oh! And there you are.

CHERRY. Sorry, Miss. I thought I'd get you a few bits, while you was out. I got you a walking stick at the Supermarket.

> (**CHERRY** *hands* **MISS MARPLE** *a walking stick.*)

MISS MARPLE. Oh. Thank you.

CHERRY. And I found a lovely bit of mackerel. It's amazing what they got, all in one shop.

DOLLY. I gather they expect you to take a basket and go round and pick out all the food *yourself*. And they call it progress.

MISS MARPLE. Oh Dolly, do be quiet. *(To* **CHERRY.***)* If you bought everything from one shop, why have you been so long?

CHERRY. …

MISS MARPLE. I'm afraid Mrs Bantry saw you this morning.

DOLLY. Waiting for a *bus*.

(Beat.)

CHERRY. Well, it doesn't matter now, cos you've worked it all out.

I went to the film studios. I saw him. Cut the cable to the lamp. That butler.

MISS MARPLE. Thank you, Cherry.

CRADDOCK. I'll call you once we've brought him in.

*(**CRADDOCK** leaves.)*

DOLLY. I suppose you suspected all along.

MISS MARPLE. I knew Miss Gregg was protecting someone but…

*(**MISS MARPLE** suddenly looks at **CHERRY**.)*

Why *were* you at the studios?

CHERRY. I – I'm just such a big fan of hers and I…

MISS MARPLE. Ah. Of course.

(Gentle.) So that's why you moved here? To see her again.

Charlotte.

CHERRY. …How did you…?

MISS MARPLE. I should have guessed right away. You were so upset.

CHERRY. She was my mother, all them years, and she didn't even…

MISS MARPLE. No one looks past a uniform.

DOLLY. My God! You mean, you're one of Miss Gregg's…

CHERRY. Abandoned kids, yeah.

DOLLY. *(To **MISS MARPLE**.)* I did tell you Cherry wasn't a real name. I mean, Cherry Baker, how ridiculous.

CHERRY. I went to talk to her at the studio, but then I saw Giuseppe make that lamp fall, right where she'd just been sitting! I told that secretary, and she said she'd tell the police, but no one did anything, so I thought, I'd have to tell them, but they'd think it was strange, me being at the studio, so I spent today all in a dither, and all I could think, if I didn't say anything and she died...

MISS MARPLE. You've been very brave.

CHERRY. Why didn't the secretary tell the police?

(An aggressive knock at the door. They freeze. A second aggressive knock.)

MISS MARPLE. *(To* **CHERRY***, quietly.)* Does anyone know where you live?

CHERRY. No. Why?

MISS MARPLE. *(Indicating back door.)* Go home. Out the back way.

CHERRY. But –

MISS MARPLE. Now!

(Beat. **CHERRY** *scarpers. The sound of the front door opening.* **GIUSEPPE** *rushes in.* **DOLLY** *grabs the stick. Holds it up defensively.)*

GIUSEPPE. No, I... I want to speak to Miss Baker.

MISS MARPLE. I'm afraid she's gone.

GIUSEPPE. Gone? Where?

MISS MARPLE. Well, I wasn't really listening –

GIUSEPPE. Where did she go?

MISS MARPLE. She did tell me but these days, I'm afraid, I get so confused. *(To* **DOLLY**.*)* She didn't say anything to you, did she?

*(***DOLLY*** shakes her head. Unable to speak.)*

GIUSEPPE. When is she coming back?

MISS MARPLE. Who, dear?

GIUSEPPE. Cherry. Your help.

MISS MARPLE. Oh, now I recall! She said she was going to Gossington Hall.

> (**GIUSEPPE** *turns on his heel, goes.* **DOLLY** *lets out an almighty sigh of relief.*)

DOLLY. I thought he was going to kill us, right here!

MISS MARPLE. Oh, Dolly! You were so brave.

I'm so sorry I told you to be quiet.

DOLLY. You were very clever, Jane, sending him straight into the arms of the police.

MISS MARPLE. I only hope Cherry gets back all right.

DOLLY. I'm sure she will. Thanks to you.

Is there anything Mr Craddock has actually done to contribute to the solving of this crime?

MISS MARPLE. Now Dolly, that isn't fair.

DOLLY. Whenever I look at him, I keep remembering that dreadful investigation, and the toll it took on my poor Arthur.

MISS MARPLE. You must miss him so.

DOLLY. It's better now I'm in the cottage. I couldn't bear it at Gossington. His chair. His place at the dining table. His side of the bed.

MISS MARPLE. You were very courageous to move.

DOLLY. Jane, I... I didn't sell Gossington out of choice. By the time I'd paid off all the death duties, and the debts and the fees and – I've never been very good with money... And nor, it turns out, was Arthur.

MISS MARPLE. You should have told me.

DOLLY. But you haven't got a penny to your name either!

MISS MARPLE. I just meant, I would have understood.

(Beat.)

DOLLY. I think, after all this, we deserve a nice cup of tea.

MISS MARPLE. Or something stronger.

*(**DOLLY** smiles. Helps them both to a sherry.)*

DOLLY. I thought it was Miss Zielinsky.

MISS MARPLE. That sneeze could have been deliberate. And *(Delicately.)* in love –

DOLLY. Oh! With Mr Rudd.

MISS MARPLE. With Miss Gregg. It does happen, you know.

DOLLY. Good God! How on earth does that work? Actually, don't tell me.

*(**DOLLY** downs her sherry.)*

I wish I were clever like you.

MISS MARPLE. I'm not clever. I just know what people are like, that's all.

Do help yourself.

DOLLY. *(Pouring herself another drink.)* I ought not to be too long. Lucy said she'd pop in later.

MISS MARPLE. Oh, lovely. How is she?

DOLLY. ...Now I've had a glass of sherry, perhaps I can admit... I never liked to talk about my children in front of you. In case you minded.

MISS MARPLE. How can I miss something I never had? Though that was very thoughtful of you.

DOLLY. D'you know, I spent the first ten years wishing they'd leave me in peace. And now they have.

MISS MARPLE. But you often visit them.

DOLLY. And they put up with me. But they have nothing to say to me, except "do you remember when..." And sometimes, I don't.

MISS MARPLE. Oh Dolly, they adore you.

DOLLY. I did love it so. But I was always so terrified, that Wilfred would never learn the seven times table, or that Lucy wouldn't sit with her knees together.

Isn't it odd, that sex makes babies? They're such terribly different things to do.

(Beat.)

The house. It was dreadfully quiet without them.

How have you managed, all these years?

MISS MARPLE. I used to see life branching out in front of me, one possibility and then another, and another, and now I see a brick wall.

DOLLY. Good Lord, you've only sprained your ankle. And you've solved a whole murder! If there is a brick wall, I think you just hurdled over it.

MISS MARPLE. I wonder why Marina Gregg didn't send for her girls when she was better?

DOLLY. Perhaps she thought it wouldn't be fair to uproot them again.

MISS MARPLE. Perhaps... Or, if not, I expect that's what she believes now.

We're meant to forget, but the idea of being forgotten, it's...

DOLLY. I've never forgotten your Lawrence. He had the most smashing smile.

MISS MARPLE. You can't have been more than seven.

DOLLY. I always had an eye for the boys.

MISS MARPLE. Larry's been gone for forty-four years and three months... And he still pops up in my dreams.

DOLLY. Is that why you never...met anyone else?

MISS MARPLE. Dolly, I... The telegram said he'd been shot for cowardice.

I never told anyone.

DOLLY. Oh Jane...

MISS MARPLE. I learned later that he'd had – shellshock, they call it now. The court martial lasted twenty minutes.

When it came to it, a man – a boy, really...the boy executed for cowardice refused to wear a blindfold.

I always think of the Kipling.

"I could not look on Death, which being known,

Men led me to him, blindfold and alone."

And now look. We live in a world of Showers and Supermarkets.

(The sound of police sirens.)

DOLLY. I expect that means they've got him.

MISS MARPLE. I expect so.

(Beat.)

DOLLY. I really ought to run along. *(Gently.)* Lucy promised she'd bring the latest addition.

MISS MARPLE. Oh, good. I just finished these booties, for the baby.

*(**MISS MARPLE** holds out knitted booties.)*

DOLLY. Oh, Jane.

(**DOLLY** *takes the booties. Both a little choked up.*)

I'll pop in first thing.

(*A moment.* **DOLLY** *goes.* **MISS MARPLE** *sits there. Something's not quite right.*)

(*More police sirens. Then, the telephone starts to ring.*)

(**MISS MARPLE** *crawls determinedly towards it.*)

MISS MARPLE. Wait, wait, wait!

(*She gets there. Picks up the telephone.*)

(**CRADDOCK** *appears, at Gossington Hall. He's on the telephone, not wanting to be overheard.*)

St. Mary Mead, 395.

CRADDOCK. Giuseppe Renzo has been murdered.

MISS MARPLE. But...

CRADDOCK. So not the culprit after all.

MISS MARPLE. Where was he –

CRADDOCK. Shot. In the grounds.

MISS MARPLE. He came here... I sent him back to Gossington.

CRADDOCK. To his death.

(*Beat.*)

MISS MARPLE. Perhaps someone put him up to releasing the lamp... And then killed him, so he couldn't give them away! Unless Cherry *was* lying...

CRADDOCK. You mean, you might have been wrong about Miss Baker?

MISS MARPLE. What about the knife and the picture? Did you dust those for fingerprints?

CRADDOCK. Of course we bloody did! Nothing!

MISS MARPLE. What about Miss Zielinsky! Cherry told her what she saw at the studio. But she didn't mention it to you, did she, which seems / very –

CRADDOCK. / I should never have shared confidential information with you –

MISS MARPLE. Or perhaps she told Mr Rudd and – Insurance! Did you look into the film insurance?

CRADDOCK. There's a proper process for a reason!

I'll come and visit next time I'm in the area.

MISS MARPLE. Dermot, I –

> (**CRADDOCK** *puts the phone down. Leaves.*)
>
> (**MISS MARPLE** *crawls back to her chair. She hauls herself up. Only then notices the crutches and stick.*)

You bloody old fool.

> (**MISS MARPLE** *sits in silence for some time.*)
>
> (*Darkness begins to fall.*)
>
> (**MISS MARPLE** *reaches for her knitting. It's a struggle. Eventually, she retrieves it.*)
>
> (*She can't even face knitting.*)
>
> (*She cries.*)

(She reaches for her handbag. Takes out her compact. Powders her nose. Her fingers trace the wrinkles, a blemish...)

(She stops still. A blemish. She thinks, and thinks, and thinks.)

Oh Lord... That would... [make sense]

Oh no...

(Urgently, she grabs her stick. Hobbles to the telephone. Dials. **DOLLY** *appears, with her telephone.)*

DOLLY. Mary Mead, 373.

MISS MARPLE. Dolly, it's me.

DOLLY. I heard more sirens!

MISS MARPLE. Mr Renzo. He was killed.

DOLLY. But you said he was the killer... *(realising what's happened)* Oh, Jane!

MISS MARPLE. I have to put this right.

DOLLY. You were just trying to help. There's nothing wrong with wanting to feel useful.

MISS MARPLE. Kettles are useful.

When Heather Leigh told that story about queueing to get Marina Gregg's autograph, what did Heather say she had come down with?

DOLLY. Oh, not this again.

MISS MARPLE. You mean, you can't remember.

DOLLY. I mean, a man has been killed –

MISS MARPLE. I thought you got rather a thrill out of that sort of thing.

DOLLY. No. That's you.

> *(Beat.)*

MISS MARPLE. Look, you said Heather Leigh had a rotten head cold, when she met Miss Gregg all those years ago, but that wouldn't make any sense, because she said she covered it with make-up –

DOLLY. So?

MISS MARPLE. I think it might be important that you remember exactly what was said.

DOLLY. How can I remember when you're hounding me?

MISS MARPLE. I'm sorry. I thought there was a chance I could put things right.

DOLLY. Chicken pox?

MISS MARPLE. Ah. Never mind then.

> *(We see **GIUSEPPE**.)*

(Distraught.) We sent that poor man into the arms of a killer!

DOLLY. You mean, you did.

MISS MARPLE. Yes.

He must have come here to warn Cherry.

Which means if Cherry told Miss Zielinsky, then Miss Zielinksy is in danger too.

> *(We see **ELLA**, holding some flowers.)*

DOLLY. Measles. German measles.

MISS MARPLE. Oh dear. Yes, I feared it might be that.

DOLLY. I don't...[follow].

MISS MARPLE. We had better get ourselves to Gossington Hall, right away.

Scene Two

*(**ELLA** is putting down some flowers. She sneezes. Fumbles for her atomiser.)*

*(**MISS MARPLE** appears, with her stick, out of breath and in pain.)*

ELLA. How did you get in?

MISS MARPLE. I know the previous owner. Are you… feeling all right?

ELLA. Couldn't be better. Why?

MISS MARPLE. Oh, I am glad.

ELLA. What are you doing here?

MISS MARPLE. I came to warn you –

*(**ELLA** sneezes.)*

ELLA. Where's my goddamn –

*(**MISS MARPLE** sniffs. Detects something unusual.)*

*(**ELLA** finds her atomiser. She goes to inhale.)*

Stop!

Forgive me. May I… *(Indicates atomiser.)*?

*(Beat. **ELLA** hands **MISS MARPLE** her atomiser. **MISS MARPLE** sniffs it.)*

MISS MARPLE. Oh, that's very clever.

*(**ELLA** sneezes. **MISS MARPLE** wraps the atomiser in her handkerchief.)*

ELLA. Hey –

MISS MARPLE. Is it true that Miss Baker told you she saw Mr Renzo release the lamp?

ELLA. ...Why?

MISS MARPLE. Why didn't you tell the police?

ELLA. Marina said she'd handle it.

MISS MARPLE. And that didn't strike you as odd?

ELLA. She always gets Jason to deal with this stuff – oh God. You don't think... Jason? But he was with Lola and me when the lamp – *(Realising she's implicating herself.)* Hang on, you think I'm in on it?

MISS MARPLE. Of course not. But you need to tell the Chief Inspector what you just told me. Oh, and that someone just tried to kill you too.

ELLA. What?

MISS MARPLE. I think you had better hurry, my dear. Miss Gregg really needs our help.

(Beat. ELLA goes. MISS MARPLE takes a moment. Hobbles through to:)

Scene Three

(Marina's room. **MARINA**, *alone with her thoughts.)*

*(***MISS MARPLE** *outside, alone with her thoughts.* **MISS MARPLE** *steels herself. Goes in.)*

MISS MARPLE. I'm afraid I have some very bad news for you –

MARINA. What are you doing here? Who let you in?

MISS MARPLE. Your husband is about to be arrested for double murder, and the attempted murder of Ella Zielinsky.

MARINA. Jason? No! No, it wasn't him. It can't have been.

MISS MARPLE. I'm very sorry.

MARINA. Wait! You said "attempted murder". Ella, is she… all right?

MISS MARPLE. I got to her in time, yes.

MARINA. *(Best acting ever!)* Thank God.

And is everyone else…okay?

MISS MARPLE. I presume you're asking about Cherry.

MARINA. I'm afraid I don't know what you mean…

MISS MARPLE. The girl serving the drinks at the party.

She calls herself Cherry, although her real name's Charlotte.

(Beat.)

MARINA. How dear.

MISS MARPLE. As it happens, I haven't seen her today. Not since the studio.

(Beat.)

MARINA. What is it you want? To be part of a murder investigation? Or to be part of our lives?

MISS MARPLE. Ah, fame! It draws people in, like moths to a light.

The trouble with that, one so easily gets burned.

MARINA. The trick is never to take yourself too seriously but rather to be grateful, for every day people still mistake you for a star.

MISS MARPLE. Your world makes my little life seem very drab indeed.

(Beat.)

MARINA. Why don't you come to the studio again? You can watch the filming whenever you like. And parties. There are always so many parties and – I'd be thrilled to have you there as my honoured guest.

MISS MARPLE. It is beguiling, I grant you –

MARINA. Excuse me?

MISS MARPLE. But it must get very wearing for you, having to put on that face all the time.

MARINA. I was blessed with a wonderful gift. It's my duty to try to make people happy.

MISS MARPLE. How kind. But I have no interest in being part of your world.

MARINA. So why are you here?

Miss…

MISS MARPLE. Marple. Jane.

MARINA. I can see you're very lonely, Jane, and I'm sorry you weren't invited to yesterday's party. I'd only just got here, and someone else made up the VIP list. Next time, I personally shall see to it that you –

MISS MARPLE. It won't work on me. But I am trying to help you.

MARINA. For the bearer of bad news, you seem very pleased with yourself.

MISS MARPLE. No. I am very aware of where I have fallen short.

MARINA. I'm sure that's what you tell yourself.

MISS MARPLE. And you?

MARINA. Come on. Be honest. Why are you really here?

MISS MARPLE. You know why I'm here.

MARINA. No. You're not here to help.

You want recognition.

   (Silence.)

MISS MARPLE. *(Floored.)* ...I don't...

MARINA. And you call me beguiling?

   (Silence.)

MISS MARPLE. Perhaps we're not so different.

MARINA. And? [Am I supposed to be offended?]

MISS MARPLE. Except that I didn't adopt and then discard two children.

MARINA. Is that the best you can do?

MISS MARPLE. At the party, you didn't even recognize them!

   (Beat.)

MARINA. Them?

MISS MARPLE. Lola Brewster's real name is Alice. It took me a while to work it out too but then, I had never met her before.

(Silence.)

MARINA. The waitress...is she really Charlotte?

MISS MARPLE. Yes.

MARINA. Is she...safe?

MISS MARPLE. I sent her away.

(A moment. **MISS MARPLE** *waiting for* **MARINA** *to give herself away.* **MARINA** *remains inscrutable.)*

*(***CRADDOCK*** appears. He sees* **MISS MARPLE**.*)*

CRADDOCK. What the hell are you doing here?!

MARINA. Is my husband with you?

(Beat.)

CRADDOCK. I'm very sorry, Miss Gregg.

MARINA. Can I see him?

CRADDOCK. I'm afraid I can't permit that.

MARINA. Please, Chief Inspector. Allow your procedure a little slack, just this once.

CRADDOCK. He's under arrest.

MARINA. I know.

MISS MARPLE. Let her see him. One last time.

(Beat. **CRADDOCK** *relents. Turns to go.)*

Oh, and Dermot. Can you get your men to track down Cherry and bring her here?

CRADDOCK. What?

MISS MARPLE. That would be most helpful, dear.

MARINA. Please, Chief Inspector…

> *(Beat.)*

> *(***CRADDOCK*** exits.)*

> *(***MISS MARPLE*** and ***MARINA*** alone together.)*

MISS MARPLE. Well?

Will you tell them what you have done, or will I?

MARINA. How would it help anyone, to know?

Or would it just help you…? For the world to know you were the only one who worked it out?

> *(Silence.)*

> *(***LOLA*** enters.)*

LOLA. Marina, I wanted to tell you– *(Seeing* **MISS MARPLE.***)* Oh. Excuse me. I'll come back another –

MARINA. Alice…?

Is it really you?

> *(***MARINA*** goes to touch ***LOLA****'s face.* ***LOLA*** pulls back.)*

LOLA. I wrote to you, for years! Why didn't you…

MARINA. I never got your letters… I was told you didn't want anything to do with me.

LOLA. I thought…

MARINA. No. If I'd known…

LOLA. I did this film to find you, but you just looked right through me…

MARINA. I'm so sorry. My darling girl.

(**MARINA** *opens her arms.* **LOLA** *does not go to her.*)

(**CRADDOCK** *appears, with* **JASON**, *guarded by a* **POLICE OFFICER**. **ELLA** *follows.*)

Jason! This is Alice! I've found her! I've found my daughter!

JASON. Oh, Marina! Marina...

(*They embrace.* **JASON** *makes his decision.*)

MARINA. Please, Chief Inspector. It can't have been Jason –

JASON. (*Stepping up; lying.*) I lied, Inspector. It *was* me. All of it was me.

MARINA. No...

JASON. (*To* **MARINA**.) I know this must be a shock but I did it because... (*Emphatically.*) There is a woman I love very much and I wanted her to have the life she deserved.

Don't say anything. Just let me go and they'll leave you in peace. You and your daughter.

CRADDOCK. And, once you've been found guilty, I presume Miss Gregg will inherit the money.

MARINA. What money?

CRADDOCK. If this film collapses, the insurance pay-out is twelve million dollars. (*To* **JASON**.) But I expect you hadn't mentioned that to Miss Gregg. Had you?

ELLA. You did all this for money? You bastard.

JASON. I did this...for love.

(**MARINA** *goes to him, takes his hand. They gaze into each other's eyes.*)

CRADDOCK. All right. Take him / away –

> *(Interrupted by **DOLLY** appearing, with **CYRIL**.)*

What are you doing here?

DOLLY. I found Mr Leigh, loitering outside.

CYRIL. I do not loiter! *(To **CRADDOCK**.)* Inspector Craddock, I really need to –

CRADDOCK. Not now, man!

> *(**CRADDOCK** turns back to **JASON**. **CYRIL** and **DOLLY** wait, overlooked, as **MARINA** won't let **JASON** go.)*

Miss Gregg... He tried to *kill* you.

MISS MARPLE. And he'll hang for it.

Unless...

> *(**MARINA** clings to **JASON**.)*

> *(**CRADDOCK** coughs. **MARINA** peels herself away. **CRADDOCK** nods to the **POLICE OFFICER** – take him away. **MISS MARPLE** looks at **MARINA** ... Can she really do this?)*

MARINA. All right.

LOLA. Mommy?

MARINA. But you all have to understand...

> *(The scene replays again but this time, exactly as it was. **HEATHER** and **MARINA** both hold drinks. **JASON** beside **MARINA**.)*

HEATHER. Oh, Miss Gregg. I know you won't remember me but –

MARINA. I meet so many dear people –

HEATHER. *(Earnest, endearing.)* Of course. Sorry. You must get this all the time. Someone telling you a silly story about how they met you once but I wanted to tell you... I've never done anything with my life. Not like you.

MARINA. I'm sure that's not true.

HEATHER. Well, I helped with the night watch, in the war, but – the point is, when I see you, in the pictures, you make me feel so *alive*... Like there's a whole world out there that's so beautiful and... Sorry. What I'm trying to say is – when you came to play Cleopatra, I waited for hours, though I nearly didn't go 'cos I wasn't very well –

MARINA. You are sweet –

HEATHER. The doctor told me to stay in bed but I didn't feel too bad – it was only German measles – so I put on lots of make-up and you came right up to me and gave me your autograph and you even let me kiss you. It was thirteen years ago but I carry that moment with me every day...

> *(Focus falls on **MARINA**, her face frozen in terror. Music.* The sound of a mirror, shattering.)*

Because you made me feel as if I actually matter.

Sorry. I didn't mean to – are you all right?

> *(**JASON** equally appalled, quickly gathers himself.)*

JASON. Honey?

> *(**MARINA** snaps back, puts on her best smile.)*

MARINA. How kind of you to go to so much trouble.

---

* A license to produce *The Mirror Crack'd* does not include a performance license for any third-party or copyrighted recordings. Licensees should create their own.

HEATHER. I didn't mean to prattle on, it's just it meant such a lot to me.

MARINA. Do excuse me. I have to... *(Looking around, sees* **LOLA.***)* say hi to my co-star.

> (**MARINA** *smiles, leaves with her drink.* **JASON** *and* **HEATHER** *look at each other awkwardly.*)

JASON. So. What does the Saint Johnny's Ambulance actually do?

> (**LOLA** *goes up to* **MARINA.***)*

LOLA. Hi. Do you remember me now?

MARINA. Sure. It's Lola, right?

LOLA. ...Right.

Your house, it's so –

MARINA. I'm sorry, I don't recall actually inviting you...

LOLA. You didn't. I wanted to say hi, again, away from the filming...

MARINA. Sure. You've said it now, sweetie.

LOLA. Marina... I...

MARINA. Yes?

LOLA. I wanted to tell you... I hoped we might be friends.

MARINA. I don't have friends.

> (**MARINA** *makes her way to* **ELLA.** **CHERRY** *was about to go up to* **MARINA** *but loses her nerve.* **DOLLY** *intercepts* **MARINA.***)*

DOLLY. Oh Miss Gregg, who knew such wonders could be created from porcelain?

> (**MARINA** *smiles, distracted. Keeps heading to* **ELLA.** **HEATHER** *beckons to* **CYRIL.***)*

HEATHER. Cyril! Stop loitering in the corner! Come and meet Mr. Rudd. He's a film producer!

JASON. Director.

(CYRIL reluctantly joins HEATHER.)

(MARINA turns away, putting the Calmo in the glass she still holds, as she makes her way to ELLA.)

MARINA. What are my duties after the party?

ELLA. You'll be meeting the Vicar, the head of the Women's Institute and –

MARINA. And plenty more crazy fans!

ELLA. Want me to rescue you?

MARINA. I'll be nice for another couple of minutes, make her happy, and then, maybe you could come and get me.

ELLA. Sure. Oh, your necklace...

(ELLA lovingly readjusts MARINA's necklace.).

(MARINA smiles graciously. GIUSEPPE intercepts MARINA on her way back to HEATHER.)

GIUSEPPE. I heard what that woman said. Please, don't – [do anything]

MARINA. Later, honey... Please?

(Beat. GIUSEPPE goes back to his position as MARINA rejoins JASON and HEATHER.)

JASON. – known of her work for years but it was at a party, a mutual friend and –

MARINA. I'm so sorry. Ella was listing my duties. So, Mrs, um –

HEATHER. Leigh –

MARINA. Of course. How long have you lived in St Mary Mead?

> (**ELLA** *sneezes. We focus on* **MARINA**, *deliberately jogging* **HEATHER**'s *elbow.* **HEATHER** *spills the drink all over* **MARINA**'s *dress.* **HEATHER** *looks mortified.*)

HEATHER. I'm so sorry – your poor dress –

MARINA. I never liked it anyway. Oh, but your drink! Now, you must have my drink and I'll get another –

HEATHER. Oh no, I couldn't –

MARINA. No, really. I insist.

> (**MARINA** *hands* **HEATHER** *her drink.* **HEATHER** *takes it, smiles.*)

HEATHER. You really are just as lovely as I remembered.

> (**HEATHER** *drinks. The effect is almost instantaneous. She swoons.* **CYRIL** *catches her.*)

CYRIL. I'm so sorry – she doesn't usually drink. Heather, my love? Heather? Heather? Help!

JASON. Get an ambulance. Quick!

CYRIL. Heather?

DOLLY. (*Fumbling in her handbag.*) I might have some smelling salts…

> (**CYRIL** *is trying to bring her round.* **ELLA** *tries to help, but –*)

ELLA. She's dead.

> (**ELLA** *snaps back to:*)

(*To* **MARINA**.) Oh my God! It was you!

LOLA. I don't understand…

MISS MARPLE. If a woman catches German measles during the first four months of pregnancy, it can have a serious effect on the child.

MARINA. …I never knew how I'd caught it, and there she was…so…proud.

LOLA. So…the baby died?

MARINA. He was badly brain damaged. Because of that woman. And then he died, six months ago.

LOLA. …Why didn't you tell us…? We would've helped you.

MARINA. …They said I couldn't look after him; that, in the eyes of the world, he wouldn't even exist. And all his problems were caused by my catching German Measles.

MISS MARPLE. It wouldn't have occurred to Heather Leigh that the doctor told her to stay at home not for her own sake but for the sake of everyone else.

I should have seen sooner… But everyone said something different. *(To* **MARINA**.*)* You told us that Heather Leigh had been suffering from influenza.

DOLLY. And I hadn't a clue!

MISS MARPLE. Memory is malleable. Besides, you got there in the end.

I think Cherry knew all along, and that she deliberately threw us off the scent.

*(***CHERRY** *appears/steps forward.)*

CHERRY. I didn't see nothing.

DOLLY. Anything.

MISS MARPLE. Exactly. A very clever use of the double negative.

DOLLY. Oh, I see!

MISS MARPLE. What I think she *did* see was Miss Gregg managing to make Heather Leigh spill her drink, all over Miss Gregg's dress. I assumed Cherry wasn't the brightest, snob that I am whereas really –

CHERRY. And she spilled her drink all over her dress...

MISS MARPLE. Every word, chosen with care.

DOLLY. *(Working it out.)* She...spilled *her* drink...all over *her* dress. Oh, now that is clever.

MISS MARPLE. Cherry – who didn't like to lie.

CHERRY. Sorry I'm late. I can't think of an excuse.

MARINA. ...Charlotte protected me...?

LOLA. What? Charlotte? Is she here?

MARINA. *(Upset.)* She was the waitress. I didn't even...

LOLA. Me neither! *(Doesn't know whether to laugh or cry.)*

(Excited.) So, where is she? Where's my sister?

> *(***MARINA*** can't answer. She looks at* ***MISS MARPLE.****)*

MISS MARPLE. Giuseppe came to find her, so I sent her home. I'm sure the police will bring her here.

Poor Giuseppe saw the whole thing too, I presume.

MARINA. He always saw everything. He offered to help me. To make you all believe that someone really was after me. He found the knife in some purse; it was his idea to plant it with the picture of me, and –

CRADDOCK. It *was* Giuseppe who released the lamp.

MARINA. Yes.

> *(We see* ***GIUSEPPE*** *release the studio lamp.* ***CHERRY*** *sees the whole thing. Gasps in horror.)*

MISS MARPLE. Poor Charlotte. She'd seen the deliberate spill… But seeing Mr Renzo cut that cable… She must have been terribly confused.

CRADDOCK. So why didn't she tell the police?

(**MISS MARPLE** *looks to* **ELLA**.)

ELLA. She told me about the lamp, and I said I'd tell them but –

(**ELLA** *takes* **MARINA**'s *hand.*)

I'll take care of it, okay? I'll tell the police and –

MARINA. No!

ELLA. They have to know –

MARINA. Of course. Just – not yet, okay? Give me some time.

ELLA. You're not safe. If Giuseppe tries again –

MARINA. I need you to trust me here… Don't think I don't see it, the way you care for me…just as I care for you…

(**MARINA** *strokes* **ELLA**'s *face.*)

ELLA. You…care for me?

MARINA. You know I do. I've got this, Ella, darling. Just, don't say anything to anyone yet. All right?

(**ELLA** *nods.* **MARINA** *kisses* **ELLA**. *Turns back.*)

Oh, who was it who saw? So I can thank them.

ELLA. A fan, I guess. Here, she left her details. Cherry Baker.

(**ELLA** *interrupts, brings scene back to:*)

Oh God…

DOLLY. Oh! So that's why you sent Mr Renzo to find Cherry!

LOLA. You sent Giuseppe, to kill Charlotte...?

MARINA. I didn't know! I didn't know!

MISS MARPLE. And when he came back empty handed –

(Dark. Eerie. The shadows of trees. **GIUSEPPE** *appears.)*

MARINA. Did you do it?

(**GIUSEPPE** *hands the gun to* **MARINA**.)

GIUSEPPE. I would do anything for you – [but]

MARINA. Giuseppe...sweetie...

GIUSEPPE. It is impossible. Either I live with your secrets crushed against me, or I live knowing I am the one who sent you to the gallows.

MARINA. You promised you'd never tell a soul...

GIUSEPPE. The other woman, I understand how much she hurt you. But this girl...?

MARINA. What are you saying?

(Beat.)

GIUSEPPE. I will leave now, though it will pain me the rest of my years, not to walk where you walk. But I swear to you, I will never speak a word, not to a soul, not anyone.

MARINA. I want to believe you...

GIUSEPPE. You know I love you. I have always protected you.

MARINA. Protected me? From what?

GIUSEPPE. The gossip, newspapers, the letters –

MARINA. What letters?

GIUSEPPE. Alice and Charlotte, they wrote, again and again. I got rid of the letters.

MARINA. ...You told me they wanted nothing more to do with me.

GIUSEPPE. You asked me to keep you clear from all that. And Mr Rudd, he –

MARINA. He meant from stories getting out! Not from my daughters!

GIUSEPPE. I didn't know –

MARINA. How could you do that to me?

GIUSEPPE. I lie to everyone for you. Your husbands, newspapers, the police. And now, you ask me to kill a girl! All these years, I put up with your shit, thinking I'm the lucky one, but look at you. Look at who you really are.

>   (**GIUSEPPE** *grabs for the gun. In the tussle, it goes off.* **GIUSEPPE** *falls.*)

MARINA. No. No... I didn't mean to... Giuseppe.

>   (**GIUSEPPE** *is dead.* **MARINA** *cries.*)

I really didn't mean to.

MISS MARPLE. Did you mean to put the rat poison into Miss Zielinsky's atomiser?

>   (**CRADDOCK** *looks at* **MISS MARPLE**. *She gives him the atomiser.*)

ELLA. You tried to kill *me*?

MARINA. I didn't want any of this...

ELLA. At least Giuseppe doesn't have to spend the rest of his life knowing how little you actually cared for him.

MARINA. I care... I care...

>   (**ELLA** *walks out. Turns back. Looks at* **MISS MARPLE**. *Seeing her anew.*)

ELLA. You saved my life.

*(Beat. Then **ELLA** goes.)*

CRADDOCK. *(To **MARINA**.)* Why didn't you just confess? Wouldn't it have been simpler than having to…

MARINA. What's more simple than the desire for life? And death. It overwhelms everything.

… *(To **JASON**.)* Did you know, all along?

JASON. I didn't want to believe it. But I heard what that woman said, knew what it meant and… I know how much you loved your boy.

MARINA. You wanted me to let you hang for me.

JASON. I love you.

MARINA. You've made every decision for me.

JASON. I try to make life easier for you, that's all.

MARINA. You can't medicate shame.

You brought me here, to help me forget. I don't want to forget Sam. How could I ever forget that I abandoned my son?

JASON. I thought, if you could just…start again… and acting, it always made you happy…

MARINA. What is happy? I mean, without the care of family, what are we?

JASON. I'm your husband.

MARINA. I'm just an image in a magazine, on a poster, a screen… I've only ever been what you imagine me to be.

JASON. You're a beautiful woman –

MARINA. And when I'm not?

JASON. Marina –

MARINA. "Beauty" doesn't cure anger. And it doesn't cure grief.

CRADDOCK. You're not the only one who has lost the person they love. It does not turn us all into murderers.

MARINA. I think I became a murderer the second I discovered what caused my son's condition.

(Silence.)

MISS MARPLE. I cannot put my hand on my heart and say that, had I found myself in your position, I too would not have done the same.

(Silence.)

LOLA. I wish I'd known.

MARINA. I do love you, Alice. I always did.

You will tell Charlotte, won't you? Tell her I...

*(**LOLA** flings herself into **MARINA**'s arms.)*

My darling girl...

And Jason...

I'm so sorry I wasn't the woman you wanted me to be.

JASON. No. I'm the one who should be sorry. All these years, I thought I was the only one who really knew you, but you're right... I saw a delicate woman, tearing herself apart, standing still... and I thought, if I just cleared the path before you, you'd find where you wanted to go... but all I was doing was sending you in the direction that I had chosen for you. I never stopped to ask you. Maybe, because I was scared that if I did, the answer wouldn't be me.

MARINA. I was never delicate.

JASON. Yes. I know that now.

I see you, Marina. And I will love you, to the grave.

MARINA. Oh, Jason... It would always have been you.

> (*They look at each other. Finally seeing each other. Too late.*)

MARINA. Promise me something?

JASON. Anything.

MARINA. Live your life to the absolute fullest when I've gone.

> (**JASON** *tries to nod yes but he can't bear the weight of grief to come.*)

MARINA. (*Looks to them all.*) You too, Alice... And tell Charlotte. All of you. Make the very most of your lives... for me; for poor Mrs Leigh; and for my darling Samuel...

> (**MARINA**, *the star, till the very last moment, gathers herself. This is it.*)

(*To* **CRADDOCK**, *with dignity.*) May I go put my face on, one last time?

> (**CRADDOCK** *nods.*)

> (**MARINA** *turns to go. Turns back.*)

Miss Marple... Jane. You were right. It's not so much recognition as the need to matter.

MISS MARPLE. Yes. I think that's it, entirely.

> (**MARINA** *and* **MISS MARPLE** *look at each other. Mutual understanding.*)

> (*Beat.* **MARINA** *leaves.* **JASON** *goes to follow He stops. Turns to* **CRADDOCK**.)

JASON. May I...?

> (**CRADDOCK** *looks helplessly at* **MISS MARPLE**. *She gives a small nod.*)

CRADDOCK. Yes.

> (**JASON** *exits.*)
>
> (**CHERRY** *bursts in.*)

CHERRY. Oh Miss, I lied to you. Well, I didn't really lie but –

MISS MARPLE. We know. Now, Cherry. There's someone I'd like you to meet –

CHERRY. You know?

MISS MARPLE. Well. Find, really.

CHERRY. What?

LOLA. Charlotte...

CHERRY. Bloody Nora. Alice?! I didn't...

LOLA. Me neither.

> (*They rush to each other. Embrace.*)

CHERRY. Where did they send you?

LOLA. Chicago. You?

CHERRY. Croydon.

> (*Beat. They laugh.*)

Bloody 'ell! You're a ruddy film star!

LOLA. I thought it would be the best way to reach her. Mommy.

CHERRY. Where is she?

> (**LOLA** *shakes her head. Can't say.*)

MISS MARPLE. Charlotte, dear. I know that you saw her deliberately spill that drink.

CHERRY. I was gonna tell you, but then... (*Indicates* **CRADDOCK**.).

I heard that she was coming here so I got a little bedsit, set meself up as a help to pay me way, and I was gonna surprise her, but then I saw her deliberately spill that drink. I didn't know what to do cos I still love her, don't I, but then I saw Giuseppe cut that light, so I thought maybe I'd got it wrong but – *(Looks at* **MISS MARPLE**.*)* but you'd already worked all this out, hadn't you? I knew it, that you was as quick as a fish.

MISS MARPLE. And I should have realised you were.

CHERRY. But I live on the Development.

> *(Beat.)*

(To **LOLA**.*)* Why did she do it?

LOLA. You will understand.

CHERRY. She'll be hanged, won't she?

> *(Silence.)*

Can I see her? Before she…

CRADDOCK. She's upstairs.

> *(Beat.)*

CHERRY. *(To* **LOLA**.*)* D'you wanna come?

LOLA. I've made my peace. I'll be outside, when you're done.

> *(***CHERRY** *turns to go.)*

CHERRY. *(To* **MISS MARPLE**.*)* Miss… Thank you.

> *(A moment.* **CHERRY** *goes.)*

MISS MARPLE. Look after yourself, my dear.

LOLA. I will. You too.

> *(***LOLA** *leaves.)*

CRADDOCK. I got it wrong. Again.

MISS MARPLE. So did I. But we got it right in the end.

CRADDOCK. You did.

MISS MARPLE. I couldn't have done it without Dolly.

> (**MISS MARPLE** *turns to her friend.* **CRADDOCK** *realises* **DOLLY** *and* **CYRIL** *have been there all along.*)

Perhaps you should walk Mr Leigh home, after everything he's been through.

CYRIL. Yes. I'm still here.

CRADDOCK. I'm so sorry. I didn't...

CYRIL. Notice me?

I lost my wife and it didn't occur to any of you to ask me what I saw, what I suspected...

People like Heather and me, you think so little of us, you can't imagine that anyone would care enough even to want us dead.

My one consolation is that Heather would've died happy. Meeting that woman all those years ago was the most exciting thing that ever happened to her.

> (**CYRIL** *remembers, and we see, all those years ago,* **HEATHER** *putting powder on her face to cover the German measles.* **CYRIL** *reading poetry.*)

HEATHER. Does my rash show? Do I look all right?

CYRIL. No. I mean, Yes. I mean, you look lovely *(Smiles.)*.

HEATHER. Are you sure you won't come?

CYRIL. I've got a date with T.S. Eliot.

HEATHER. Or you could do those shelves. Oh, and don't forget you said you'd creosote the step. And the door to the larder's come loose, again.

(He puts his book down. Laughs.)

Sorry. I don't mean to go on.

Are you sure you don't want to come, my love?

CYRIL. More your thing than mine.

*(**HEATHER** clutching her autograph book. Turns to go. Turns back.)*

HEATHER. I've never been so excited!

CYRIL. You're much more beautiful than some film star.

HEATHER. Don't be stupid. I'm just some nobody.

CYRIL. No. You're not. Not to me.

HEATHER. I do so love you, Cyril Leigh.

*(She kisses him. Goes. **CYRIL** now alone, in the present, distraught, leaves.)*

MISS MARPLE. *(To **DOLLY**, gently.)* Dolly… Take him some sherry.

DOLLY. I'll pop over later. Help you to bed.

MISS MARPLE. Dolly…

DOLLY. Don't say anything else or I might cry.

*(**DOLLY** goes to **CRADDOCK**. Uncertain. Then pats him consolingly on the shoulder. Leaves.)*

CRADDOCK. How did you know?

MISS MARPLE. I know people, that's all. And I've seen so much evil. It comes from living in a village my whole life.

And Dolly talked about that poem, *The Lady of Shalott*. Do you know it?

CRADDOCK. I read it years ago. I don't... [remember...]

MISS MARPLE. It's about a woman imprisoned in a tower, condemned to weave a tapestry; the reflection in her mirror, the only link to the outside world. If she turns to face the world as it really is, she will bring about her own death. And of course, one day, half-sick with shadows, she dares to look down, and sees a man she could have loved... At that moment the mirror cracks and the web unravels; and she realises that she is doomed to die.

Dolly talked about that *look* and I thought – I *assumed*, Miss Gregg must be frightened of *someone*. But then after Giuseppe's death, I put it all together and... I realized I hadn't considered that it might be a look of fear of herself and what she was surely about to do.

(Beat.)

CRADDOCK. Jane, I... Did I really used to have accidents?

MISS MARPLE. What? Oh. No, I'm afraid I made that up to flush you out.

CRADDOCK. ... *(Smiles.)* You were very good to me when Mother died, and...

MISS MARPLE. I'm sorry too.

(Beat.)

CRADDOCK. I'll see this through and then, if you'll permit me, I'll run you home.

MISS MARPLE. And I'll open the port and tell you about the time your mother and I happened to have tea with Charlie Chaplin.

CRADDOCK. Yes. I'd like that.

(A moment.)

MISS MARPLE. "Doomed to die." You don't suppose…

CRADDOCK. Oh God.

> (**CRADDOCK** *turns to rush off but before he can exit,* **JASON** *enters, ashen-faced,* **CHERRY** *behind him.* **JASON** *carries an empty glass. Beat.*)

JASON. She's dead. *(Cries.)*

> (*Beat.* **JASON** *offers* **CRADDOCK** *the empty glass.* **CRADDOCK** *hesitates.*)

CRADDOCK. *(To* **JASON***.)* Was it you?

JASON. She made her own choice, this time.

> (*He looks at* **MISS MARPLE**.*)*

Thanks to you.

> *(A moment.)*

(Cries.) But I didn't stop her.

> (**CRADDOCK** *looks to* **MISS MARPLE**. *What to do? She holds his gaze.* **CRADDOCK** *softens.*)

CRADDOCK. Probably best not to admit that.

> (**JASON** *looks to* **MISS MARPLE**, *helplessly.*)

MISS MARPLE. He's right. You've been through enough.

CRADDOCK. At least Miss Gregg has been spared the public humiliation.

MISS MARPLE. I don't know. I'm sure she would have done very well on the stands.

But now, we must tell her story for her. With kindness, grace, and forgiveness, for everything each one of us got wrong.

MISS MARPLE. *(Softly.)* No one is ever just one thing. A murderer. A nobody. A spinster. We have all, at times, been guilty of failing to look properly but now… Marina is right. We must live our lives all the better for knowing her, and all those who have gone before.

> *(**JASON** bows his head. Sobs. **CHERRY** sobs too. **MISS MARPLE** holds out her hand to **CHERRY**. **CHERRY** takes **MISS MARPLE**'s hand.)*

(Quietly.)

"He said, 'She has a lovely face;

God in his mercy lend her grace,

The Lady of Shalott.'"

The End

www.ingramcontent.com/pod-product-compliance
Ingram Content Group UK Ltd.
Pitfield, Milton Keynes, MK11 3LW, UK
UKHW041007200625
459870UK00011B/162